Cool-inary Moments

Culinary Memories, Mishaps, and Masterpieces
Including Real Recipes
Flavored with a Little Advice

COMPILED AND EDITED BY YVONNE LEHMAN

GRACE PUBLISHING

Royalties for this book are donated to Samaritan's Purse.

COOL-INARY MOMENTS
Culinary Memories, Mishaps, and Masterpieces
Including Real Recipes Flavored with a Little Advice

ISBN-13: 978-1-60495-037-3

From Samaritan's Purse

We so appreciate your donating royalties from the sale of the books *Divine Moments, Christmas Moment, Spoken Moments, Precious Precocious Moments, More Christmas Moments, Stupid Moments, Additional Christmas Moments, Loving Moments, Merry Christmas Moments* and now, *Cool-inary Moments* to Samaritan's Purse.

What a blessing that you would think of us! Thank you for your willingness to bless others and bring glory to God through your literary talents. Grace and peace to you.

Their Mission Statement:

Samaritan's Purse is a nondenominational evangelical Christian organization providing spiritual and physical aid to hurting people around the world.

Since 1970, Samaritan's Purse has helped victims of war, poverty, natural disasters, disease, and famine with the purpose of sharing God's love through his son, Jesus Christ.

Go and do likewise.
Luke 10:37

You can learn more by visiting their website at
www.samaritanspurse.org.

DEDICATION

Dedicated to
Terri Kalfas, who saw the beauty
and value of sharing praise in
Divine Moments
Christmas Moments
Spoken Moments
Precious, Precocious Moments
More Christmas Moments
Stupid Moments
Additional Christmas Moments
Why? Titanic Moments
Loving Moments
Merry Christmas Moments

and

to the 47 authors who shared 58 stories
for this compilation
without compensation
just for the thrill of being useful
and being part of the mission work of
Samaritan's Purse
who receives all the royalties
from the sale of these books

TABLE OF CONTENTS

INTRODUCTION

LIVER SPOTS

I took the liver out of the freezer and put it in a colander in the kitchen sink to thaw. When I returned to check, it was thawed so I put it on a plate but saw tiny grayish-white spots all over it. It smelled like good liver, but I knew it was diseased, as if it had chicken pox. I showed it to my husband who agreed we'd have to throw it out, rather than take a chance on us and our four children eating chicken-poxed liver.

Through the years, I occasionally cooked liver and always thought of that diseased liver, wondering what had infected it. Had the entire calf been diseased? Had anyone been poisoned?

About twenty or so years later, I was rinsing raw vegetables and watching the water run through the little holes in the colander. Suddenly (well...not exactly suddenly...it had taken twenty years), it dawned upon me what caused the liver spots.

As the liver thawed, the softness pressed against the holes in the colander, causing little bumps devoid of blood. That changed the texture and color of the otherwise perfectly healthy liver. Had I waited a while, the blood would have re-colored the gray spots.

Moral of the story: Don't judge your liver by its poxes — leading to...Don't judge the cooks in this book by their mishaps in the kitchen.

Be thankful you have a kitchen, and food (even if it sometimes turns out inedible).

Jesus asked God's blessing before feeding the 5,000
and gave thanks at the Lord's Supper

When I was a child, I was taught to fold my hand together, fingers tipped up beneath my chin, bow my head, close my eyes, and say:

God is great, God is good.
Let us thank him for our food.
By his hands we all are fed.
Give us, Lord, our daily bread.
Amen

Okay, so we might be ones about whom it is said, "She can't boil water without burning it." I wouldn't know about that. The water I boiled wasn't there by the time the smoke alarm went off. The bottom had burned out of the pot and the metal was stuck to the burner of the stove.

Ah well, there's more than one way to cook a goose.
Or… roast a reindeer.
Or… thaw your liver.

Enjoy the mishaps, the yummies, and the Forever Food.

Yvonne

1

THE THINK BLESSING

Praying aloud in public is a problem for me. I attribute it to memorized prayers. Therefore, I decided to teach my children to make up their own prayers.

The first comment was from my four-year-old who said, "I can't thank God for worms. They don't taste good."

The first *homemade* prayer came out, "Thank you God for frogs."

It was terribly difficult to keep my composure. I lectured myself on the value of frogs, trying to picture them as cute, sitting on a lily pad; but for the life of me I could only visualize a deep-throated "crruuump" and a warty, scaly, bulgy-eyed, long-tongued fly catcher.

By trial and error, I learned to guide my children in their prayers, like, "When we're eating vegetables it would be nice to thank God for vegetables and save the frog and worm prayer 'til you're outside…etc."

The oldest, Lori, understood, and my second child, Lisa, presented no problem because she always copied Lori.

As the years passed and we added David and Cindy, other problems arose. The baby, Cindy, always chimed with squeals of delight at having folded her hands, which often drove the other three into hysterics. Finally, the activity simmered down to applause (A little enthusiasm before meals isn't too bad!) and eventually graduated into hand folding and mumbling.

They soon became so enthusiastic that it became a daily fight about who was going to say the blessing. They would rush to the table screaming, "first-first!" and the first to scream was "it."

In our family no one wants to be second. So it often ended in hurt feelings (usually in my hands), accusations of "she was first last time," pouting, being sent to bedrooms, then eventually a half-hearted duty-blessing.

So, we developed a plan whereby each child was scheduled the same day each week. I carefully explained that when one says the blessing, the others can be second, third, etc. if they wish, or the others can "think" a blessing.

They seemed to go for the idea of thinking a blessing. I explained that God knows what we mean when we think it. We do not always have to pray aloud.

I was amazed at the response to the "think" blessing. With one blessing rather than six (my husband and I had our turns too), we were able to eat hot meals again.

One night, after putting the children to bed for the last time and turning out the light, I returned to the living room for my nightly deep sigh of relief.

After a few moments the patter of little feet interrupted the silence and Lisa stood before me, very calm and self-satisfied.

"What are you doing up?" I asked sternly.

She answered in all seriousness, "I can stay up. I thinked it."

Sometimes I'm a little slow so I asked the inevitable. "You thinked what?"

"I thinked going to sleep, and God knows what I mean, so now I can stay up."

...atleastitsneverdull...

Yvonne Lehman

2

BAKING WITH MOM

My mom and grandma knew how to bake.
I especially liked their cookies and cake.
Recipes handed down through time
Now become my daughter's and mine.
The flavors of their baking, I recall with affection,
Memories of bygone years, with reflection.

Mom made a cookie she named "Peter Pan."
Out came peanut butter, then the work began.
She blended and mixed the ingredients well,
Dropped dollops onto a pan, to let them swell.
Fork imprints flattened her cookies slightly,
When baking, each cookie expanded rightly.

Cookie sheets filled, but we couldn't partake.
Mom shoved them into the oven, to bake.
The aroma of the freshly baking goods
Whiffed throughout our neighborhoods.
Placed on a rack, waiting to be cooled,
Pleasurable delight — my taste buds ruled.

Mom offered one cookie, saying, "That's enough."
But waiting 'til after lunch would be tough.
She left. I tip-toed to where those cookies were
Slipped my fingers into that big cookie jar.
I schemed. Just-one-little-bite. My heart sang.
"Stop," called Mom, who heard the jar lid bang.

Carol A. Baird

3

Achoo!

Back when I was a young, spry woman, I loved to cook. The process consumed many pleasant hours as I crafted dishes from scratch to impress my dinner guests.

On one such occasion, I decided to prepare my favorite spaghetti sauce recipe. The kitchen resounded with singing as I chopped onions, diced peppers, browned authentic Italian sausages, added fresh tomatoes from my garden, and sliced garlic. For hours everything cooked together perfectly to create a fabulous sauce. I added wine, salt and pepper, and my Italian spices to the mix and allowed the magic to happen in the pot as I prepared salad and a dessert. Of course, I set the table well in advance with my best dishes and candles.

By the time my guests arrived, I was exhausted, but exhilarated. I loved serving a fabulous meal.

The spaghetti reached al dente perfection and I scooped it onto a huge platter. I then dipped the sauce on top. It was beautiful and smelled amazing.

My guests sat at the table watching me with wide eyes, and perhaps a bit of drool, as I carried the platter to the table, my head held high. Just as I reached the powder blue carpet of the dining room, I felt a sneeze coming on. The black pepper had finally reached my sinuses.

I didn't have time to get to the table and put the platter down, but I did have time to turn my head far enough that when the explosion came, I managed to avoid contaminating my spaghetti masterpiece with my, "Achoo!"

I smiled with relief as I turned back to my friends, only to find them all with even wider eyes and dangling jaws staring at...an empty platter.

At my feet, and covering a good portion of the powder blue

carpet, the entire platter of spaghetti and sauce lay like the remains of a gluttonous drunk's dinner.

Tears dripped from my eyes as I scooped up the remnants of my day's effort and tossed it in the trash. Even after successive scrubbings, the tell-tale orange stain remained to taunt me every day we lived in that house.

At least we ate the salad and dessert I had prepared — and the pizza that arrived about thirty minutes later. My guests assured me I would, "laugh about it…someday."

Guess I'm still waiting for that someday!

I never made homemade spaghetti sauce again.

But…ready for some good ol' Appalachian Fruitcake?

Karen Lynn Nolan

Appalachian Fruitcake

Karen Lynn Nolan

Ingredients

2½ cups flour

2 cups sugar

1½ teaspoons soda

1½ teaspoons salt

¼ teaspoon baking powder

1 teaspoon cinnamon (or more)

1 teaspoon cloves (or more)

½ teaspoon allspice

1½ cups applesauce

½ cup water

½ cup shortening/butter

2 eggs

1 cup raisins (soaked in warm water and drained)

½ cup chopped walnuts (add more) English or black

mixed candied fruit

Directions

1. Preheat oven to 350°.

2. Grease and flour baking pan (preferably an angel food pan).

3. Measure ingredients into large bowls (separate bowls for wet and dry ingredients).

4. In a third bowl, combine ingredients by alternately adding dry/wet/applesauce and mixing after each addition.

5. Add fruit, nuts, raisins and blend ½ minute on low speed, scraping bowl occasionally.

6. Pour into pan.

7. Bake 60-65 minutes. If doing layers, bake for 50 minutes.

8. Cool before removing from pan.

4

MUD PIE LESSONS

My cupcakes had pretty leaf designs on them today," I announced to my parents when they picked me up at my grandmother's home. During my grade school years, I was allowed to stay with her for a few hours or overnight. She lived in a modest house with few personal possessions. Her lack of stuff, though, did not limit her inventiveness in making my time with her fun and educational.

I never made any baked goods with my grandmother. She only had the bare necessities for fixing meals. I didn't realize until years later, though, that she incorporated cooking lessons in my mud-pie fun time.

She kept old tin muffin pans, pie plates, a flour sifter and chipped bowls on her back porch for me to use making mud pies. I had great fun mixing the dirt with water and then pretending this was special baked goods for her and me. She delighted in my culinary creations.

I dug up dirt from the garden, dumped it into the sifter and then cranked it so only fine dirt went into my mixing bowl. The rocks and dirt clumps were deposited in a corner of the garden.

"Oh no, the cupcakes have cracks in them," I reported to her. I had been playing Chinese Checkers and forgot about my latest cooking project.

"You have to remember to watch your baked goods or they will over bake," she told me.

"Why is it taking so long for my pies to harden?" I asked on another day. "I've been waiting a long time."

"Were they in the shade of the tree? If the heat isn't hot enough, it takes much longer to bake."

"You have too much liquid in your mixture," she told me one time as I stirred the dark brown concoction. "Your pies won't be ready before you go home."

A large hackberry tree behind her house provided berries and nuts (bumps from the leaves) to add variety to the cakes. If I put in too many berries and nuts, the mixture would crumble when I tried to remove the cakes from the pans.

"We can give your cakes some variety, if you want," she told me another day as I headed out to the back porch. "Let's find some leaves to put on top of your cakes for decoration. That will make them attractive for your guests." After that I decorated my pies and muffins with grass, leaves, and seeds. I enjoyed seeing the different designs I could make on them.

"Always clean up after your cooking so the pans are ready for use the next time," she reminded me after we had "eaten" my newest creation. That wasn't what I wanted to hear; I was ready to go swing on the front porch.

When I got married, my baked goods were made with flour, sugar, salt and flavorings. Grandmother's ideas and advice were put in use for improving my culinary efforts. I'm thankful for the cooking instructions I received via mud pies.

Helen L. Hoover

5

KEEP IT MOIST

At one time in my life, I had a sweet tooth for carrot cake with cream cheese icing. Since one wasn't going to fall out of the sky, I was going to have to make my own. In my twenties and not that great a cook — gravy was a mystery and biscuits were a lardy challenge back in the day when my biscuits had some lightweight fluffy heft to them — one thing I did know how to do with relish, and that was bake cakes.

When I was twelve and needing some extra cash, I used to bake cakes for my mother's friends' dinner parties. They loved my cakes. Those ladies enjoyed singing my praises and always asked my mother how I managed to always bake such a moist cake. "However does she do it — could you ask that little darlin' for us?"

"The trick," I shared with Mother, "is to undercook the cakes five minutes. But don't reveal the secret of my success." Of course Mother let the cake out of the bag. And still, the orders kept pouring in.

So, since I was a cake-baking prodigy at twelve, how hard would a carrot cake be at twenty-something? I found a trusted cookbook and combed the pages, looking for a beaut of a carrot cake.

Found one!

I measured. Broke eggs. Stirred. Blended. Dumping in the rest of the ingredients, I wondered about this recipe that would have me grate orange peels to throw into the mix. Hmmmm. So it would be an interesting carrot cake with that bright-colored zest from a citrus fruit. But one I couldn't wait to sink my teeth into. I was creating what looked to be the most magnificent carrot cake ever baked on planet earth.

Sticking the pans into the oven, I began working on the cream cheese icing. Once the cake had cooled, I swirled the thick icing between layers, on top, and around the sides. No naked cakes for me or my family and friends — lots of icing it would be. I was a "shower me with sugar" kind of gal.

And then the first bite.

Wait a minute. This tasted nothing like carrot cake. This. Was. Something. Else. Wait a minute. I never grated carrots to put in the cake. Wait a minute. That's because the recipe never *called* for carrots! How can a carrot cake not have carrots in it? Arggghhh!

Yanking the cookbook back down to take a closer look, I turned to the photo of the beautiful carrot cake, ran my index finger across the page opposite with the recipe, and there it was. In huge letters at the top of the recipe's directions: Williamsburg Orange Cake.

This was no carrot cake! I spent all that time, making that cake from scratch, only to have my taste buds shiver from culinary shock because what I put in my mouth tasted nothing like *carrot cake!*

Disappointed to the nth degree, at least I was able to laugh at my mistake. For maybe two seconds. Long enough to grab my car keys to run out and buy me a piece of carrot cake which was never moist enough to even come close to one of my cakes. If I'd only chosen the correct recipe.

Later, after the desire for carrot cake had faded, I discovered the Williamsburg Orange Cake was incredible. So instead of sharing a carrot cake recipe, I'm sharing the Williamsburg Orange Cake recipe from Oxmoor House – which is also simply divine. Don't forget to shave off five minutes of cooking time and just note that butter (not cream cheese) is used to make the icing. You can substitute a cream cheese icing if you prefer.

Now I've given away my baking secret. Keep it moist!

And read directions carefully. (A bell should go off in your brain when grating orange zest for carrot cake. There is a similarity between zest and carrot gratings, but all similarities end once the first bite goes past the lips!)

Vicki H. Moss

WILLIAMSBURG ORANGE CAKE

Vicki H. Moss

Ingredients

2½ cups all-purpose flour
1½ cups sugar
1½ teaspoons baking soda
¼ teaspoon salt
1½ cups buttermilk
½ cup butter, softened
¼ cup shortening

3 eggs
1½ teaspoons vanilla extract
1 tablespoon grated orange
  zest
1 cup golden raisins, chopped
½ cup finely chopped pecans
orange peel and sections

Directions

1. Preheat oven to 350°.

2. Combine first 10 ingredients. Blend with an electric mixer 30 seconds on low speed; beat 3 minutes on high speed. Stir in raisins and pecans.

3. Pour into 3 greased and floured 8-inch round cake pans.

4. Bake at 350° for 30 to 35 minutes or until a wooden pick inserted in center comes out clean.

5. Cool in pans 10 minutes; remove from pans, and cool completely.

6. Spread Williamsburg Butter Frosting (recipe follows) between layers and on top and sides of cake.

7. Garnish cake with orange zest and sections.

WILLIAMSBURG BUTTER FROSTING

Ingredients

½ cup butter, softened
4½ cups sifted powdered
  sugar

1 tablespoon grated orange
  zest
4–5 tablespoons orange juice

Directions

1. Cream butter.
2. Gradually add sugar, beating well.
3. Add orange peel and juice; beat until smooth.

6

WAITING FOR THE SMOKE TO CLEAR

Cooking and eating is one of the main activities in the nursing home where I work. The residents often complained about the food fixed by our dietary department.

As the Activity Director, I discussed the issue with my staff on how to better meet the residents' needs, and decided to offer them a choice once a week. It would be a dish they didn't normally get but would like to have. The residents began to request a variety of foods. The staff also joined in by planning interesting dishes.

One Tuesday, my assistant who usually does the cooking was out and I was on my own. I'm not the best cook and decided on something easy that could be fixed in the microwave. I choose to make pierogis and a peach pastry.

I put the pastries on a pan and stuck them in the little oven in our office. Following the directions on the package, I cooked six pierogis in the microwave without any trouble. They turned out beautifully and I was proud to serve them to those gathered around the activity table.

Then we had additional residents join our group, so I put two more pierogis on a plate and stuck them in the microwave. I set the timer for six minutes, as I had with the first batch, and walked back into the activities room.

I thought something smelled strange, but I couldn't figure out what it was. I went back to check on how much time was left on the microwave. Smoke was coming out of the appliance.

I quickly pressed the stop button and opened the microwave door. The pierogis were burned to a crisp. I stood there in astonishment, trying to figure out what I'd done wrong, as the room filled with smoke.

Apparently, two pierogis did not need the same amount of cooking time as six.

A moment later a loud buzzing sound began. I'd set off the fire alarm. The doors automatically closed throughout the facility and the staff gathered in the public areas. They all stood around, wondering if it was a fire drill. I went into the commons area and told them what happened and there was nothing to worry about. "I set off the alarm."

Several staff members entered the activities room, inspecting the area, opening doors and talking with the residents.

"Are you okay?" the Director of Nursing asked one resident after another, and asked if they needed to go outside because of the odor and smoke.

None of them wanted to leave. They were enjoying their pierogis snacks that hadn't burned.

After we opened doors and windows, the smoke dissipated. However, the odor lingered in the office for another week. Then it was gone and the incident apparently forgotten.

I did not forget it, however and needed to learn from that mishap. There's a quote by Vincent Van Gogh that says, "There may be a great fire in our soul yet no one ever comes to warm himself at it, and the passers-by see only a wisp of smoke."

That brought to mind what Jeremiah said, *"If I say I'll never mention the LORD or speak in his name, his word burns in my heart like a fire"* (Jeremiah 20:9 NLT).

When cooking, I don't want there to be a foul odor or a wisp of smoke. But in my spiritual life, I do want it to be obvious to others that there is a fire for the Lord in my soul and I want them to feel invited to that warmth.

Diana Leagh Matthews

7

GRANDMA'S
COOKING LESSON

My culinary experience began in my grandma's kitchen in 1950. At age seven, I looked into the soft brown eyes of a refined Swiss-born woman who gathered me in her arms each time I visited and immediately led me to her kitchen.

"Schatzi, come, come we make the crepes now."

I always ran ahead of her. I remember I thought Grandma talked kind of funny and I was glad when my daddy explained that Grandma and Pop came from another country and they were working hard to speak English. Daddy told me that Schatzi meant "sweetheart" in their country.

Grandma waved a hand toward the kitchen. I started to run to the table where I saw the red, blue and yellow striped bowl already full with the dry ingredients.

"Wait Schatzi, put the bib on." She waved an apron toward me. I stopped to let her put it over my head and tie the straps behind my waist.

Grandma's hand trembled when she pointed to the milk. "Quick Schatzi, pour the milk. My hands not so steady anymore." She said that every time. (Grandma also used to tell me in the "old country" the milk came from Gracie, the cow.)

I poured the milk, oh so carefully. I watched it swirl through the mixture. Then Grandma nudged my shoulder. "Now Schatzi, you add the butter slowly, the eggs, and vanilla." She handed me the whisk.

This was my favorite part. I grabbed it and brought it back and forth through the dough. Then I made quick little circles turning my wrist just like Grandma taught me.

By this time, Grandma already stood at the stove heating more butter in a skillet. "Schatzie, quick, bring the bowl."

I picked up the bowl with both hands and stood behind Grandma. She always cautioned, "Back Schatzie, very hot." She never failed, during this whole process, to tap me on the nose and leave a smudge of flour on it.

I held my breath as she took a ladle. She scooped up just the right amount of mixture. When it hit the skillet, she rotated the skillet this way and that until a thin film of the mixture coated the sides. Then she gingerly loosened the edges before she flipped the crepe. As each crepe turned golden brown, grandma placed it in a stack on a large plate that matched the colored bowl. It was my job to place a piece of wax paper between each crepe.

"Schatzie, take the plate now to the table. Grandma's coming. I bring applesauce and sweetened strawberries from the icebox."

I thought it was funny that Grandma called the fridge an icebox. I waited for her to sit down before I reached for the stack of crepes.

"Schatzi, wait! You know we must first thank the Lord for our blessings and the crepes." She always admonished me softly and sweetly before she prayed.

"Here we go again, Lord. We thank you for these delicious crepes. I thank you for my beautiful granddaughter." Her chin lifted to the ceiling. "She is sorry that she wants to eat so quickly. Amen."

Grandma reached for the beat up tin can with the holes in the top. She sprinkled powdered sugar over the top of the stack, dipped a finger in the middle and tapped my nose with another white smudge.

That's how I learned how to make scrumptious crepes, but most of all, how I learned to give God the glory for everything in my life, especially Grandma and flour-tipped noses.

Alice Klies

GRANDMA'S CREPES

Alice Klies

Grandma never measured, so I had to ask her for approximates when I grew up.

Ingredients

1½ cups flour (She took a coffee cup from the cupboard: "One and a half of these.")

2 big spoons of sugar

some baking powder (I put in ½ teaspoon.)

some salt (I put in ½ teaspoon.)

enough milk for a thin batter (It almost always takes 2 cups.)

some butter (I put in a big tablespoon.)

sprinkle of vanilla

3 eggs

Directions

1. Mix all dry ingredients together, then add the butter, eggs, and milk. Stir until very smooth.

2. Heat more butter in a cast iron skillet (works best) and when bubbles start to form, pour a small amount of batter in the skillet. Right away, you must tilt the skillet this way and that until the batter reaches the sides. Watch carefully and begin to loosen the edges and flip so both sides get golden brown.

3. You may stack them individually between wax paper and serve them with sweetened fruit or homemade applesauce.

4. Be sure top to them with powdered sugar shaken from an old tin can with holes in it!

8

TURKEY IN THE RAW

One Thanksgiving dinner stands out in neon lights in my memory bank. It can bring a blush to my cheeks, even forty-five years after the fact.

My husband's father passed away in the spring of 1972. I knew the first holiday without him would be difficult for my mother-in-law. She had not been adjusting well to a life without her spouse. What better way to help our children's grandma through Thanksgiving than to gather her three sons and their families at our house for the day? Five of the seven grandchildren were preschool age, and two were slightly older. The house would be filled with children playing, adults talking and the soothing balm of a turkey dinner. We'd make this a good holiday for Grandma. I issued the invitations via phone and began to plan a special day.

By Thanksgiving Day, I'd baked and done the pre-cooking. Now the turkey, filled with a moist sage stuffing, roasted in the oven. White potatoes, candied sweet potatoes, cranberry sauce and a green bean casserole were close to being ready. Nutmeg and cloves scented the corner of the counter where the pumpkin pies cooled.

"When do we eat? When do we eat?" the kids pleaded more than once.

I consulted the scrap of paper where I'd jotted down the amount of time the turkey needed. "Pretty soon," I told them.

The aroma of the roasting meat added to our hunger, and I placated the entire clan with sodas, juice, and appetizers and some adult beverages.

Finally, it was time to take the turkey from the oven, and what a beautiful bird it was — big, browned, and beckoning. I called my brother-in-law, known as Best-Carver-in-the-Family, to the kitchen. One sister-in-law mashed potatoes while the other made gravy. Toddlers scurried around us yelling, "Is it time now?"

My husband and his oldest brother were glued to a football game on TV. Grandma sat stone-faced on the sofa, looking miserable. As I was trying to move the little ones into the family room, my brother-in-law uttered words that sent a chill straight to my bones. "This turkey isn't done. It's raw in the middle."

Silence reigned. No one said a word, but all eyes were on me. The question, "Well, what are you going to do now?" reverberated in my head. What does a person do with a partially cooked turkey, side dishes ready for the table, and a houseful of hungry people?

I flew into action. First, I put the cover on the roaster, popped the bird back into the oven, and turned up the heat. Lids went on the already cooked dishes and we fixed hot dogs for the children, who probably enjoyed them more than the big dinner anyway.

An hour later, we resurrected the turkey, reheated the side dishes and sat down to eat, minus hot-dog-stuffed children. The seven adults gathered around our dining room table ate to satisfaction and then some.

The children appeared like magic when the desserts were served. Grandma managed to eat her dinner and join in on the conversation, not exuberant but not crying. I felt like she was counting her blessings, for many of them sat nearby.

The family togetherness took precedence over all other things. I'd planned the day so that Grandma would be surrounded with those she loved, and it didn't really matter that I'd miscalculated the time for cooking the turkey. But I've never forgotten it, and every now and then, the story of turkey in the raw generates laughter and some good-natured teasing — one more bond within our family.

Nancy Julien Kopp

9

Smoke Alarm, Secret Pal, and Simple Things

A slightly acrid aroma alerted my olfactory senses, but it took a moment to register. Then, a high, piercing alarm rang out.

"Oh, no, the biscuits!" I raced into the kitchen, grabbed a potholder, and pulled open the oven door. Charred circles of dough reposed on a cookie sheet. I removed them from the oven, closed the door, and sighed. I placed the cookie sheet on the stove, moved to the smoke alarm, and fanned the air around it with a towel to make it stop sounding.

"What is it?" my husband called from another room.

"Burned the bread again," I replied.

No response to what was a commonplace occurrence.

As I stood waving the towel, I realized the one bright spot in my cooking fiascos was finding our smoke alarm batteries were still good.

I have somehow managed to keep my husband and two children alive with my cooking for all these years. Barely. We've had close calls, though, with my limited cooking repertoire and sketchy ability to execute recipes. My lack of culinary expertise is established and long-standing.

Years ago when I first moved to this town as a single career woman, I became friends with a young mother, Sandy. We would sit on the church steps following choir practice, and long after everyone else went home, we'd be sharing life. Thankfully, we never discussed recipes.

A short time later, her women's circle assigned her a secret pal. I wasn't in a circle at the time, so when her pal started sending her things like candles and cute kitchen towels, I felt a little jealous because Sandy was one of my few friends. She was *my* pal.

But I decided I could compete with candles and kitchen towels. I would buy Sandy a nice placemat set for her birthday. That should do it. But to my dismay, her secret pal resorted to something with which I'd never be able to compete — recipes — all kinds of complicated and wonderful recipes, the kind that take a whole page just to list the ingredients. What would I do?

I riffled through my large assortment of like-new cookbooks. (I kept buying them thinking I might find one that would change my life.) But how could I send her a recipe of something I had never tried?

Then it came to me. I bought colorful blank cards and sent her a recipe I knew she couldn't resist. Brilliant in its simplicity if I do say so myself. Here it is:

Peanut Butter Crackers

Ingredients

4 to 8 saltines

peanut butter, crunchy, or smooth (can't say how much, depends on your taste)

Directions

1. Scoop peanut butter from jar with knife and lavish on saltine.

2. Repeat four times.

3. If you like cracker sandwiches, add another cracker.

4. Enjoy!

Serves 1

Sandy loved the recipe and declared she used it innumerable times.

So, there, secret pal. Compete with that!

It's true that the simplest things in life are often the best. Take for example the simple truth of the gospel: *For God so loved the world that he gave his one and only Son, that whoever believes in him shall not perish but have eternal life* (John 3:16 NIV).

So simple, and yet it takes a leap of faith.

Sometimes, we may see the gospel as too complicated. But it's not. There's not a long formula to become a Christian. The recipe is simple: We confess our sins to God, ask his son, Jesus, to be our Savior, and follow him, allowing him to fill our lives with his love and forgiveness.

If you've not believed this simple message of God's great love, today is a good day to take that leap. Let me know if you do.

I'll be so happy; I might make you a peanut butter cracker.

Beverly Varnado

P.S. I have never been stingy with how to formulate my culinary masterpieces. Feel free to share the Peanut Butter Cracker recipe. The best news — no danger of smoke alarms.

MAKING SCRAMBLED EGGS

Someone's moving around downstairs. My nightstand clock flashes 5:27 A.M.

Jeannie awakens too. "What's going on?"

"I hear sounds downstairs."

Jeannie sits up. "What kind?"

"Footsteps. Doors banging. It's probably nothing." I slide into my slippers. "I'll check. Stay here."

Jeannie yawns. "Okay. Wake me if it's something serious." She rolls over, pulling the comforter up to her chin.

I hurry down the hall to Josh's room. He sleeps soundly, cradling his Dodgers cap. His bat leans against the dresser. My fingers curl around the handle.

The nightlight in Becca's room casts a dim glow across her vacant bed. The bathroom's empty. Again I hear muffled noises and strain to identify them. My grip on the bat tightens as I inch down the stairs, ready to fight for my family.

I open the kitchen door a crack.

Standing tiptoe on a cushioned chair in her teddy-bear nightgown, my six-year-old daughter reaches for a box of Cheerios on a shelf. Each time she stretches to grab it, her chair rolls and she totters.

I whisper, "Hi, Princess." She startles. The chair lurches. As it slides from under her, she grabs the shelf. Becca dangles, then crashes to the floor. The yellow box follows, scattering tiny O's all over the terrazzo tiles.

I drop the bat and scoop her up. "It's okay. I didn't mean to scare you. You all right?" I examine her face. No cuts or bruises.

Her mouth puckers. Her eyes mist. She stares, but doesn't cry. Then she throws her arms around my neck, hugging me. I hold her tight, rubbing her back.

"Are you okay?" I ask. She nods. She still hasn't said a word. I worry about a concussion.

Finally, she relaxes.

I seat her on the kitchen counter, kiss her nose and check her face again.

"I guess you couldn't sleep. Well, neither could I." I close the cabinet door. "So I'm glad you're here to keep me company." I push the chair back to the table. Becca watches. "Hungry?"

She nods, still silent.

"Want something warm? Cold?"

"Warm," she says. I think she might be chilled, so I toss her a sweatshirt from a nearby hook. She slips it on, hugging the long sleeves to her chest.

I sweep the stray O's into a dustpan and toss the lot into the compacter. I return the cereal box to the shelf. I don't like to cook, but I need to keep my promise to my daughter. But what to prepare that would enchant her, yet not embarrass me? "Want to learn to make scrambled eggs?"

Becca nods, rubbing her stomach.

I select two plates. "Since this is the first time you're cooking a whole breakfast by yourself, let's use these dishes to make this a special meal." I hold them out. "Put them on the table."

She places them close together. The concentric green, blue, brown and yellow rings around each rim blend with the forest green tablecloth.

"Now a fork and spoon next to each plate."

While she arranges the utensils, I grab a mixing bowl, a skillet, an extra bowl for shells and an eggbeater.

"Looks good," I say, nodding toward her place setting. "What's missing?"

"My cup."

"Right. And a glass for me. And some napkins."

Becca starts to push a chair toward the cabinet.

"Where you going?"

"I need a chair to stand on."

Oh no, I think. I pick her up and open the cabinet door. Becca grabs her tumbler and a glass and takes them over to the table.

She opens the drawer above the trash compacter cabinet.

"Where do the napkins go?" she asks, clutching a fistful.

"Mom puts them on the left of the plate under the silverware, but some put them on top of the plate. You decide."

She does it Mom's way, as I gather eggs, butter, milk, cheese, salt and pepper. Becca watches closely.

"Ready to start?" Her eager eyes and smile are all the answers I need.

I set her on her knees on the cushioned seat of a breakfast chair.

"What's first?" I ask.

"Scramble the eggs."

I move the carton closer and take out one brown egg.

"This is how you get the egg out of the shell. First you crack it hard on the flat surface of the counter." I crack the egg. "Then you separate the halves of the shell and let the egg inside fall into the bowl." The slime oozes its way into my bowl. "Then you throw the shells in this extra bowl." I dump both shells.

"Let me try. Let me try."

I hand her an egg and push the mixing bowl nearer the edge of the counter.

"I'll hold the bowl, while you crack the egg."

Becca gingerly strikes the surface of the counter, barely cracking her eggshell.

"A little harder."

She tries again, making a larger dent. Harder again. Slime oozes out, coating her fingers.

"Now grab the egg in both hands and pull the shell apart."

She does, but moves it away from the bowl. Part of it pours into the bowl, and part streams onto the counter. Her mouth puckers. Her sticky hand twirls strands of red hair, soaking them with goo. I think she's going to cry.

"No problem. I did the same thing when I was learning." I get a paper towel and clean off the counter. I don't care about her hands or her hair. "Let's try it again." I give her another egg.

This time she cracks it on her first try. She deliberately moves it over the center of the bowl. When she pulls the shell apart, the egg plops into the bowl. No fuss. No mess.

"How many eggs do you want?"

"How many are you going to eat?"

"Two" I say.

"Me too."

I hand her another egg. "We'll need four eggs. Two for each of us. Can you do that again?" Without hesitation, she cracks the first shell and dumps the egg into the bowl. Then the second and the third. She discards the shell halves into the extra bowl. No mistakes. Her face beams.

"Fantastic! You're a born cook."

She looks at the yellow goo in the mixing bowl. "Now what?"

"Now we mix."

Tilting the bowl, I turn on the eggbeater. "See, that mixes the egg to a fine consistency." I hand it to her. "Now you try it. Whip it until everything blends together."

As I hold the bowl, Becca whips. I pour in a small amount of milk. "This is fun!" she squeals.

While I light the stove, Becca lifts the beater from the bowl. She lays it on the counter and reaches in to touch the yellow batter. Becca pays no attention as egg drips on the counter and runs down the surface of the tiles. Gingerly, she tastes the runny mixture.

"Yuk!" she cries and wipes her hands on my sweatshirt. "This tastes yucky!"

I towel off her hands, dab at the counter mess and move the bowl closer to the stove. "Can you get a butter knife?"

She climbs down, extracts one from the silverware drawer, and hands it to me. I lift her back onto the cushion.

I give her the knife. "Cut a pat of butter and put it in the frying pan." She does, and I take the buttered pan to the stove.

She pushes her chair closer to the stove and climbs aboard again.

"This is the dangerous part. You could get burned if you're

not careful. Hold the pan by the handle and move the butter around to coat the entire bottom of the pan." I hold her tightly around her waist as she complies.

"See how it's starting to bubble? That means it's getting too hot." I move the pan off the burner.

"Now, while I hold the frying pan, you pour in the eggs." She tilts the bowl. The yellow stream cascades into the frying pan and sizzles. Becca's eyes widen.

"You're doing great. Pour it all in." She tilts the bowl until the last few sticky drops plop into the pan.

I move the congealed sections aside, making room for the uncooked portion.

"Okay, Princess. Your turn." I hand Becca the stirring stick. "Just keep pushing the cooked portions out of the way so the liquid can touch the bottom of the pan."

Becca stirs. Occasionally, I guide her hand to retrieve egg high on the bowl's rim. While she stirs, I add bits of Mozzarella, salt and pepper.

"Sweetie, get the plates." I take over stirring, as Becca fetches them.

I divide the eggs, flipping one portion onto Becca's plate, another onto mine. While I turn off the stove and run water over the frying pan, Becca takes our plates to the table.

Jeannie enters, awakened by the aroma.

Becca beams, confident in her new-found skills.

"Look, Mom, we made breakfast by ourselves," she announces. "We don't need you anymore."

The recipe is embedded in the article

Add: A grimace and questioning eyes

Watch for wife's smile — after she glances at the mess "someone" will have to clean up.

Frank Stern

11

A Glass of Floating Onions, Anyone?

There are some things one never lives down.

When I was growing up we always had food in the freezer so we could put together a quick and easy dinner. Things like leftovers, spaghetti sauce, fresh berries, and juice from fruits including oranges and lemons were always in there. Mom often made beef stock and chicken stock to make into a soup or stew, as well.

To make chicken stock, Mom simmered a chicken along with carrots, onions, and celery. Once the flavors had blended, she took out the vegetables. Then she put the stock in quart-sized Ziploc bags and stored them in the freezer for future use.

One day, we had company from out of town. Mom and Aunt Danielle went to a museum, leaving Dad and Uncle Wayne at home to visit with each other.

Dad wanted to demonstrate his hospitality as well as his culinary skills to Uncle Wayne, so he decided to make some lemonade. He took a yellow package out of the freezer, assuming it was lemon juice. He measured a cup of it, mixed it with a cup of sugar, and added water. He poured the mixture into glasses and they conversed while drinking the concoction.

When my mom and aunt returned, Dad showed Mom what he'd made. She looked and was horrified to see onions floating in it instead of lemon pulp. He'd made his lemonade out of chicken stock.

Uncle Wayne said he had thought it tasted funny, different from any lemonade he'd ever had, but didn't mention it because Dad had been so proud of making and serving it.

Dad said he couldn't tell the difference from usual lemonade!

Even now, thirty years later, we joke about it from time to time.

LEMONADE

Ingredients

1½ cups lemon juice
2½ cups sugar
9 cups water

Directions

1. Combine and stir until well-blended and sugar has melted.
2. Serve over ice.

Ellen Andersen

HOT DOUGHNUTS!

My husband, Larry — the ultimate sugar head — heard June 3rd was National Doughnut Day. Krispy Kreme would be giving away one free doughnut to everyone who came in. Since it would also be my birthday, he decided *we* should get one. "We should go when they open at 6 A.M. tomorrow before the line starts," he said as we climbed into bed.

"Are you kidding me? I'm going to get up before six to get a doughnut? And on *my* birthday, no less. Are you outta your ever-lovin' mind?"

Well, it wasn't six, but he managed to get me out the door and arrive at Krispy Kreme by eight.

As we pulled into the parking lot, I saw the sign. You know the one. The sign that says HOT DOUGHNUTS on the front of the building.

Then it hit me. I began to snicker. He looked at me as I said, "This reminds me of something."

"What?" he said.

"You and HOT DOUGHNUTS," I said.

He smiled, shook his head and lowered his chin to his chest.

In January 2004, Larry and I were watching the Food Network. They were talking about how Krispy Kreme doughnuts were made. When they had fresh, hot ones, they would turn on the sign announcing it in the window — HOT DOUGHNUTS. We looked at each other and laughed at how neither of us had ever heard that in all the years we had gone there. There weren't that many left in our area, so we hadn't seen them for a long time.

Until we went to Myrtle Beach on vacation in August with another family, that is. We had been to Myrtle Beach before but they hadn't, so we decided to venture up north on Highway 17 to show them around. The six of us got into our van to do some shopping, do some sight-seeing, and have supper. As we were heading back south to the condo, it happened.

The Krispy Kreme Hot Doughnuts sign lit up as we approached.

Moving down the road, going at least 50 mph, our sugar-head driver saw the sign go on. Did I mention the store was on the opposite side of the road? On Highway 17, the main drag in Myrtle Beach? It is a four-lane road with a suggested speed of 45 mph, which I'm quite positive most take it as just that… a suggestion. What happened next was truly a near-death experience.

He yelled, "Hot Doughnuts!" and proceeded to shoot across four lanes of traffic to pull into the parking lot. When I say parking lot, I mean parking spots a car length long in front of the store. He swooped across the lanes and zeroed in on a spot like a bird dive-bombing the last worm. As the van flew into the spot, we noticed the people already lined up outside, waiting to get in for their box of hot deliciousness.

A look of sheer terror spread across their faces as they tried to back up to avoid this wild man. Eyes wide open, jaws dropped, bodies plastered against the window as if they wished the glass would suck them in and they could become one with it, they were doing their best to get out of the path of the van. They looked to be climbing the window as there was no place else to go. They weren't about to give up their spot in line…but they may have toyed with the idea.

Without asking anyone else if they were coming, the sugar head jumped out and got in line. Mind you — nobody in the car had said a word. Not one word. They couldn't. If you listened closely, you would've heard five racing hearts. Five people in the car and many lined up in front of a glass window had to have thought they would be meeting each other and their Maker at that moment.

Larry climbed into the car with a huge smile and produced three boxes of hot doughnuts. He flipped open the top box and quickly pulled out three doughnuts juggling them as you would a hot potato. With a doughnut in his mouth and one in each hand, he passed the boxes to me. Meanwhile, the people in the van are still eerily silent. Without looking at any of us, he said, "Isn't anybody gonna try these while they're hot?"

Silence. One by one he looked at each of us while continuing to eat, trying to figure out why nobody was joining him in partaking of this sugary bliss.

Finally, I heard a gasp for air from the rear of the van and our daughter blurted out, "Geez, Dad, you nearly killed us. All for a hot doughnut? Was it worth it?"

Continuing to chew, he chuckled, "Yup, these are really good. Doesn't anyone else want one? I mean, I bought three dozen, surely somebody wants one." There was a long pause. Hysterics ensued and the boxes of doughnuts made their way through the van.

We have since moved to the south. There are quite a few Krispy Kreme stores around. To this day when we see a Krispy Kreme store, we have a particular ritual. First we brace ourselves. Then we look for the bright orange sign. If it's on, we yell "Hot Doughnuts!" and hold on for dear life!

I recommend you take your friends or family to find yourself a Krispy Kreme. If the sign's not on, circle around the store until it is. Once the light is on, make sure you yell, "Hot Doughnuts!" then swoop into the parking lot and get your fresh hot doughnuts. It really is worth trying them while they're hot.

Tammy Karasek

APPLE CRISP

Tammy Karasek

Ingredients

Filling

9-10 large apples (I prefer a mix of gala, granny smith, yellow delicious and honeycrisp)

¾ cup sugar
⅓ cup flour
1 teaspoon cinnamon

Topping

1¾ cups flour
1¼ cups sugar

1 cup butter (2 sticks), room temperature

Directions

Preheat oven to 400°.

1. Peel, core and slice all of the apples and place in large bowl.

2. Mix the ¾ cup sugar, ⅓ cup flour and cinnamon and pour over the apples.

3. Pour into large pie dish or a 9" x 13" pan.

4. Mix the 1¾ cups flour with the 1¼ cups sugar.

5. Cut in the butter with a pastry blender or two forks until dough is like the size of peas.

6. Spread all over the apple mixture evenly.

7. Place pie dish or pan on a large sheet pan for spillover.

8. Bake at 400° for 40 minutes until golden brown.

9. After the first 25 minutes, cover with foil so the top doesn't burn.

10. Serve warm with a side of French vanilla ice cream!

13
CHICKEN AND DUMPLINGS

When I came home from school on a crisp fall day, little stood between culinary heaven and me if the aroma of chicken and dumplings filled the air. Clear to adulthood the mere thought of Mom fixing my favorite comfort food set my taste buds to salivating. So when I called her as I was on my way to visit and she said we'd be having chicken and dumplings for dinner, I could hardly wait to get there.

Mom was finally settled into her new apartment with all the boxes unpacked and new custom-made drapes, an extravagance she still couldn't believe she owned, hanging proudly on the windows. Dad had been gone just over a year and she was moving on as best she could.

When I arrived, Mom was walking down the hallway on her way to the mailbox. I noticed she was a bit out of breath, but Mom's emphysema had been a part of our lives for many years, so her labored breathing didn't faze me much.

"There you are!" she said, as I came through the lobby door. "I can hardly wait to get started."

"Get started? You mean supper isn't ready yet?"

"No. You're making supper tonight."

"Me? You said we were having chicken and dumplings."

"We are, and you're making it!"

"B-but Mom", I sputtered. "I don't have a clue."

"Well it's high time you learned, darlin'."

I accompanied her to the mailbox and then we turned around and headed back to her apartment. As we walked down the hall, again I noticed her labored breathing. As soon as we arrived she plopped down in a kitchen chair, panting just a bit and declared with a slight giggle, "It's official Annie, I'm ... old."

"You've been saying that for the last ten years, Mom."

"Yes I know," she said. "But this time I said it's *official.*" I looked over and caught her winking at me and we laughed.

Together we chopped the carrots, onion and celery then added them along with a few bay leaves to the pot of chicken already simmering in a rich broth.

"What's next, Mom?"

"Oh, now we just wait about an hour and then the fun starts!"

While we waited, Mom and I shared a pot of tea and gabbed, catching up on family news and reminiscing about the past. She seemed content and happy with her new surroundings but I couldn't ignore the weary look in her eyes. My mom, always neat as a pin, looked run down and unkempt as she sat across from me. I thought that getting used to her new life was taking its toll on her but she'd fall into a comfortable routine soon enough.

When we finished our tea, Mom eyed the clock then peeked into the stew pot and declared with the confidence of a master chef, "It's time."

In my opinion, Mom's dumplings belonged in the dumpling hall of fame. The run of the mill kind made from rolled dough cut into squares that I'd tasted in restaurants couldn't measure up to hers in any way, shape, or form. Compared to Mom's, those were like chewing on gravy soaked rubber bands. Her dumplings started out as drop biscuit dough. By the time they bobbed to the surface of the bubbling stew, some kind of "Mom magic" transformed them into perfect puffy little tender pillows swimming in oodles of scrumptious chicken gravy.

Mom was right. I couldn't live another day of my life without learning how to do this. I watched intently as she thickened the broth with a bit of cornstarch mixed with cold water.

"Now pay attention here, Annie. This isn't hard. The important thing is to mind the pot. If you undercook them you might as well play ping-pong with them. And if you overcook them, well there's really no way to explain a sin that grave."

So I paid strict attention.

First, she whisked together the flour, baking powder, cream of tartar and a pinch each of salt and dried rosemary. Then she added melted butter and milk until the flower mixture was just moistened. The batter looked lumpy but Mom assured me that over mixing only put you on the fast track to failure.

"Lumps in the batter spell success," she said.

"If you say so, Mom. You're the expert."

Now that the batter was ready, Mom plucked two serving spoons from the dish rack and lifted a slightly heaping spoonful of dough out of the bowl. Then she used the other spoon to gently slide the dollop of dough into the bubbling gravy.

"Now you try it, Annie."

I scooped a spoonful of dough and hovered over the pot preparing to launch it, with Mom watching my every move.

"Gently, Annie! Gently! You're not shooting pool, you know. If that gravy splashes up on you, you won't soon forget it."

So I set about the task with a little more ease and a little less firing power until the dough bowl was empty.

Mom set the kitchen timer for fifteen minutes. As we finished setting the table and tossing the salad, the kitchen timer chimed. With Mom by my side I lifted the heavy cast iron lid off the Dutch oven and peeked inside. There they were, those puffy little pillow masterpieces bobbing to and fro in a sea of piping hot chicken and gravy.

"Look at that, Annie. You're a pro already."

"Well, I can't take all the credit." I said. "I had a good teacher."

Mom looked at me with her soulful chocolate brown eyes and I noticed they were brimming with tears.

"Annie, that's the nicest thing you ever said to me".

"Wow, Mom! I've never come up with anything better than that in forty-four years?"

She wiped the tears from her cheeks with a laugh and admonished me. "Don't make fun of me. I'm your mother."

We dined in style that evening with candles lit and the new

Glen Miller's Orchestra CD, that I'd just surprised her with, playing in the background.

As I was leaving the next day, Mom mentioned she'd scheduled a doctor's appointment for some time in the coming week. She said she didn't know if there was a remedy for getting old but thought it might be a good idea to see if the doctor had anything on hand. I smiled and kissed her goodbye.

Three days after my cooking lesson, Mom was diagnosed with lung cancer and lived only ninety-nine days from the date we found out.

Though she never let on, I know in my heart Mom planned that cooking lesson suspecting that her days were numbered. She wanted me to have a lasting memory that would forever bring a smile to my heart.

I learned many lessons about grace and dignity as I walked the path of those last ninety-nine days with her. But then again, I had a good teacher.

Annmarie Tait

CHICKEN AND DUMPLINGS

Annmarie Tait

Chicken Stew Ingredients

1 large broiler/fryer chicken

3 ribs of celery, sliced

5 carrots, peeled and sliced

1 large onion, diced

1 pint of chicken stock (homemade, boxed or canned is fine)

2 tablespoons of dried parsley

1 chicken bouillon cube

3 dried bay leaves (not fresh)

1½ teaspoons salt

1 teaspoon pepper

water

Directions

1. Combine chicken, celery, carrots, onion, chicken broth, parsley, chicken bouillon cube, bay leaves, salt, and pepper in a large pan or Dutch oven.

2. Add enough water to cover chicken.

3. Bring to a boil; reduce heat, cover and simmer until chicken is done (60 to 90 minutes).

4. Remove chicken and let stand until cool enough to handle.

5. Remove skin from chicken and tear meat away from bones.

6. Return meat to soup; discard skin and bones.

7. Add more salt and pepper to taste, if desired.

8. Return soup to a simmer.

Dumplings

Ingredients

2 cups Bisquick biscuit mix

⅔ cup milk

Directions

1. Mix 2 cups Bisquick and ⅔ cup milk until soft dough forms.

2. Let the dough sit for 5 minutes.

3. Drop dough by the tablespoonful onto stew.

4. Cook covered for 15 to 20 minutes.

5. Dumplings are "done" when a skewer inserted comes out clean.

14
LIES AND LEFTOVERS

I have always believed that little white lies were forgiven *if* they were told to spare someone's feelings. But I have to admit that one little white lie came back to haunt me, punishing me with great embarrassment in the process. Let me explain.

My friend, no name will be divulged, is a wonderful cook. She bakes bread, makes her own chop suey and always has a big pot of homemade soup simmering on her stove.

One of our favorite recipes that she makes is lasagna. She surprised us one night with a casserole dish filled with this delicious Italian treat.

Being busy at that moment I took the dish, thanked her with a kiss and a hug, put it in the fridge and forgot about it. I remembered about a week later when she stopped by unexpectedly. We sat down to enjoy a cup of coffee and conversation and she asked me how we liked the lasagna. That's when the little fib flew from my lips faster than you can ask, "What's for dinner?" I told her it was the best batch she'd ever made.

Here's where it came back to bite me.

Now it's a few *more* days later and my dear friend stops by again, this time looking to pick up her casserole dish. I immediately could feel my face flush to the shade of an overripe tomato as I realized it was still in the fridge — still filled with the lasagna that was never touched.

She followed me into the kitchen as I desperately tried to figure out how to save face. It was evident that my little white lie was about to be exposed.

By now her days-old specialty was starting to sprout buds of green and blue mold.

I feebly attempted to scoop out some of the contents into the sink so she wouldn't see how much was left over, but it was clear I was caught red handed when she asked, "Didn't you eat any of it?"

I'm thankful that my friend is a forgiving person. She still delights in baking and cooking for her family and, lucky for us, she still shares her specialties with us.

I have learned a valuable lesson: Being busy or not, when our friend shows up on our doorstep with dinner for two, we take the time to enjoy her culinary efforts right there and then.

And when the bowl is empty it is promptly returned, filled with our heartfelt gratitude.

Kathy Whirity

15

LOVE ON A PLATE

My grandmother moved away from Chicago about the time I started grade school but she came back to visit us for a few weeks every year. At least one time during her visit we had a Muffin Day, unannounced, and a happy surprise.

I walked the eight city blocks home from school every noontime with my classmates. It was the late 1940's, and grade school lunchrooms were never a consideration. Each day was much the same. My classmates and I laughed, chattered, and played games like Stinkfish on the sidewalk sections as we made our way home for lunch. The group diminished as, one-by-one, kids disappeared into their various houses. Mothers waited inside with lunch on the table — soup or a sandwich in most cases.

I lived farthest from school so I traveled alone on the final two blocks. The sight of our large red-brick apartment building usually made my stomach growl with hunger.

I'd walk a little faster, adding a hop, skip, and a jump now and then. Cars rumbled past on the brick street and trains that ran parallel to the road often rolled and clattered by. My degree of hunger set the pace as I ran around the bushes and green area that led to our entrance. Our vestibule doorway was one of seven entryways surrounding the formal grassy courtyard in the center of the large U-shaped building.

The moment I opened the vestibule door, I knew Grandma had made a special lunch when the aroma of hot date muffins greeted me. At the first sniff, my heart skipped a beat and I felt a flutter of excitement deep inside my stomach. My nose twitched with genuine pleasure as the scent of hot muffins floated down all three flights of stairs. My feet slid quickly across the cold, tiled entryway floor to the softer, carpeted stairs. My fingers touched the smooth stairway railing only once or twice as I flew up the steps following that ever-stronger fragrance.

I burst through the unlocked door, heading straight to the kitchen in the back of the apartment. Grandma waited there, face flushed with heat from the oven, a plate of her special muffins in her wrinkled hands.

Mother smiled at me, her delight nearly as great as mine.

"Sit down and eat while they're hot," Grandma said.

Finally, seated at the table with a tall glass of cold milk and a steaming muffin on my plate, I sniffed the delectable treat to my heart's content. The anticipation proved almost as good as the eating. Then, it was time to break the golden muffin in half and heap a generous pat of real butter on each piece. The first bite tasted of the salty butter and the sweet dates, all mingled together. Heavenly!

On this special day, our lunch consisted of as many of those treats as a stomach could hold. They were so much better than a bologna sandwich. This was love on a plate. It's a wonder that little red hearts didn't escape into the air as I broke each muffin in half. My often-stern grandmother knew only one way to show her love, and that was through the food she prepared for those close to her heart. No amount of effort, time, or cost was too big when she cooked and baked for her family.

What has kept those date muffins in my memory bank for well over half a century? Was it that they were especially delicious or that they were made with love? Perhaps a little of both. Which brings to mind my grandmother's bakery…but that's another story.

Nancy Julien Kopp

GRANDMOTHER STUDHAM'S DATE MUFFINS

Nancy Julien Kopp

Grandma mixed her muffins in a big blue crockery bowl and she always wore an over-the-shoulder Mother Hubbard apron

Ingredients

⅓ cup butter, softened

2 cups cake flour

¼ cup sugar

3 teaspoons baking powder

½ teaspoon salt

1 egg

¾ cup milk

1 scant cup dates, cut up

½ cup chopped pecans (optional)

Directions

Preheat oven to 400°.

1. Grease muffin tins, or use paper liners in the tins.
2. Cream the butter and sugar.
3. Add the egg and mix well.
4. Mix the flour, baking powder and salt together in a separate bowl.
5. Add alternately with the milk.
6. Fold in the dates.
7. Fill each muffin tin ½ to ¾ full.
8. Bake at 400° for 15-18 minutes or until done.

Makes about one dozen muffins.

Note: I substitute margarine and 1% milk to make a healthier version, and they're still wonderful. You don't even need that generous pat of butter we used "way back when."

16

AN EXPLOSIVE EXPERIENCE

Holding two-month-old Nancy in my arms, I hurried up the steps of our back porch. Two-year-old Laurie ran along beside me. I had no idea what awaited me on the other side of the kitchen door.

Stepping inside I was assaulted by an obnoxious odor. The floor was covered with shredded grayish pieces of something I did not recognize. Counter tops, shelves, table, chairs were littered with the same substance. Pieces had propelled across the half-wall separating the kitchen dinette and the living room. In the middle of the chaos was my husband, Clair.

At the same moment I saw him, I became aware that the odor was emanating from the area of the stove. A quick glance revealed a burned saucepan. It was empty. Where were the six eggs I put on to boil? I looked at Clair and asked, "What did you do to the eggs?"

The words were barely out of my mouth when I realized what happened.

Earlier that morning, Clair called to say he would come home for lunch. An appointment with a student had been delayed until later in the day. Clair taught Industrial Technology at our local community college. His schedule rarely allowed him enough time to eat with us at noon. The postponement gave him the opportunity.

"Daddy's coming home for lunch today," I told Laurie. "You can help me make egg salad sandwiches later. It's such a nice day. Let's have a picnic."

Delighted at the prospect, Laurie helped me gather the items we needed to set up the picnic table. I picked up Nancy in her Sit-and-Sleep and we went outside. Laurie watched me secure the tablecloth with metal clips. She placed the paper plates and cups on the table and started to take them out of the wrappers.

"Perhaps we should leave them in the package for now," I said. "Otherwise the wind might blow them away. Don't you think that's a good idea?" Laurie nodded. Nancy happily babbled as if agreeing.

"Carolyn," my neighbor, Karen, called from next door, "looks like a party."

I explained the reason for the picnic. She said, "Bring the girls over. Laurie can play with Beth, Mike and Amy. You and I can sit on the back steps where we can watch the kids and enjoy the sunshine."

I accepted her invitation. There was plenty of time before I needed to prepare lunch. I lifted Nancy, took Laurie's hand, and walked over to Karen's. As Karen and I chatted, preoccupied with Nancy's antics and the older children's play, the time slipped away. I suddenly noticed Clair's car sitting in our driveway.

"Goodness. I lost track of the time," I said. I called Laurie. "We need to go. Daddy's already home."

Moments later we walked through the back door to find the kitchen and part of the living room inundated with the exploded eggs. While we enjoyed the beautiful spring day with Karen and her children, I forgot about the eggs I had left on the stove.

Taking in the scene, including the incredulous look on Clair's face, it dawned on me that I was the cause of the havoc. Unfortunately, the light didn't dawn until after I blurted out my question concerning his part in the debacle. It was not helpful that Laurie, excited to see her daddy, chose that moment to run to him. As he picked her up, she pointed with a chubby finger at the floor and said, "Daddy b'oke egg."

Always calm, cool and collected in any situation, Clair was the proverbial good egg. He never became upset over any uneggspected circumstance. At times his calm demeanor could drive me crazy. This was no eggception.

He did not eggsplode over my ridiculous question placing

blame on him, which is what I would have done if the table (now covered with egg particles) had been turned. Instead of pointing out I was the one with egg on my face, he wiped the shredded pieces off the nearest chair and put Laurie down. He kissed both girls and gave me his familiar crooked grin (the one that spoke volumes without using words). He picked up his car keys and walked toward the door.

"Since there doesn't seem to be anything here to eat and I have that appointment later," he said, still grinning, "I think I'll go back to school and have lunch in the cafeteria. Their egg salad sandwiches are eggcellent."

Carolyn Roth Barnum

OLD FASHIONED BUTTER COOKIES
WITH AND WITHOUT EGG YOLK PAINT

Carolyn Roth Barnum

Bake at 400° for 5 to 8 minutes.
Makes 4-5 dozen depending on cookie cutters.

Ingredients

3 cups sifted all-purpose flour

1 teaspoon double-acting baking powder

½ teaspoon salt

1 cup butter

¾ cup sugar

1 egg

2 tablespoons cream or milk

1½ teaspoons vanilla

Directions

1. Preheat oven to 400°.
2. Mix dry ingredients together.
3. Cream butter gradually adding sugar, until creamed well.
4. Stir in egg, milk and vanilla. Add dry ingredients gradually.
5. Mix well. Chill if necessary.
6. Roll out ⅓ of the dough at a time and cut into desired shapes.
7. Place cut cookies on cookie sheets.

Stop here if using egg yolk paint & skip to *Egg Yolk Painted Cookies directions below.

Continue with these directions If Not using egg yolk paint.

Decorate cookies with colored sugar.

Bake at 400° for 5 to 8 minutes.

Or bake cookies and decorate with frosting when cool.

*Egg Yolk Painted Cookies

Place cut out cookies in layers on cookie sheet(s).

Use wax paper in between layers.

Freeze cookies in layers until needed.

To paint, remove one layer at a time for each child.

Egg Yolk Paint

Child probably should be age 2½ (if child is mature for their age) to 3+ .

Each cookie will be unique – some neatly painted as if drawing within lines.

Others will end up with a combination of whatever their painter's imagination creates.

1. Mix 1 egg yolk with 1 teaspoon of water. Divide into 4 small bowls.

2. Put 1 drop of food coloring (red, yellow, blue, and green) into each of the four small bowls of egg yolk mixture. Add an additional drop if deeper color is desired.

3. Give each child an inexpensive paint brush and small bowl of water to rinse their brush to keep colors separate as they apply different colored paint to their cookies.

4. Paint should be applied lightly to frozen cookies so brush does not penetrate thru to table

5. Bake at 400° for 5 to 8 minutes. The cookies should not be browned.

Be prepared to use separate container for storing each child's cookies. You may not be able to tell the difference, but they will.

CHOCOLATE CANDI-DATES

Ingredients

1¼ cups flour

¼ cup sugar

½ cup butter or margarine

Directions

1. Preheat oven to 400°.
2. Combine flour and sugar in mixing bowl.
3. Cut in butter.
4. Press into ungreased 13 X 9 pan.
5. Bake at 400° for 12-15 minutes until light brown.
6. Spread with warm topping.

Warm Topping

Ingredients

⅓ cup butter

¾ cup sugar

1 6 ounce package Nestle semi-sweet chocolate morsels (1 cup, divided into two ½ cup portions)

¼ cup milk

1 teaspoon vanilla extract

1 cup quick or regular rolled oats

1 cup chopped walnuts

½ cup finely cut dates (get the chopped sugar dates)

Directions

1. Melt butter at low heat in saucepan.
2. Add sugar, ½ cup chocolate morsels and milk and bring to a boil, stirring constantly.
3. Remove from heat.
4. Stir in remaining ingredients.
5. Spread warm topping on baked crust.
6. Press the other ½ cup morsels into topping.
7. Allow to cool and cut into bars.

17

Bargains and
Green Goop Dessert

When my husband Randy decided to leave his job as an executive to teach at a Christian university, our move became a journey of faith.

Confident we were following the Lord's leading, we packed and moved to another state. Even with both of us teaching, our combined salaries were less than half our previous income. Still, we left an unsold house and purchased another, carrying two mortgage payments and a bridge loan.

I began my teaching day with a 7:00 A.M. class three days a week. Randy often did the grocery shopping for the week. One day, he made an interesting discovery: On its day of expiration meat was reduced to less than half price. This was a great bargain, but only if you made it to the supermarket by 7:00 A.M. Despite glares from women at the supermarket, with an infant and a two-year-old in tow, Randy carefully selected meat for the week's menu. Our needs were met.

At the end of the school year, we wanted to host students in our home for a cookout. It was a fun idea and hard on the budget, but we knew where to purchase hamburger by 7:00 A.M. Our dessert — cookies from a nearby bakery outlet — were inexpensive. A student who worked for a soft-drink company provided cans labeled for discard because they were dented. Whenever we flip the pages of our photo album and see pictures of students holding soda cans, grilling meat and wearing wet watermelon smiles, we are reminded that God hosted our bargain picnic.

That same summer, dear friends had a campground membership and often invited us to spend time there. Our family spent many days enjoying the lake and our favorite "green goop" dessert. It was one of the best summers of our lives and our good friends lifted our spirits.

Eighteen months after our house went on the market, it sold for less than our original purchase price. In the Old Testament we read that the Israelites wandered and were fed with manna God provided. Deuteronomy 8:2 reminds us God sometimes allows us to wander in the wilderness to humble us and reveal our faith. The tax forms show that we took a loss, but we didn't. Our faith was tested and we profited from our journey. God demonstrated his faithfulness to us.

One day, we shared our stories with our Sunday school class. Good times, bargain groceries and a yummy dessert with friends at a campground were only a few examples of God's provision. Two years later, we received a note from a young bride who had attended our class. She wrote that our experiences gave her confidence that God would provide for them too, as her husband was unemployed.

Yes, God provides. Sometimes with manna, but sometimes with dented soda cans, bargain meat and green goop dessert.

GREEN GOOP

Ingredients

  2 small packages instant pistachio pudding mix
  1 large can fruit cocktail, undrained
  1 large container frozen whipped topping, thawed
  1 large can pineapple tidbits, undrained

Directions

  1. Mix all ingredients together.
  2. Refrigerate at least 30 minutes until ready to serve.

Marilyn Nutter

18

Pimento Cheese Sandwiches

In 2000 I moved to South Carolina, after a lifetime of living in Pennsylvania. Honestly, the move was initiated by the desire to no longer experience the long harsh winters that we endured annually. Living only a few miles from Lake Erie, closer to the Buffalo end, we were the beneficiaries of many, many inches of lake-effect snow.

With its hardwood trees, hilly terrain, and definite four seasons; the Piedmont of South Carolina immediately felt like home. After several years in our new location we began telling people that we weren't born in the south, but "we came here as soon as we could." We also understood that the weather might have brought us here, but the people are the reason we've stayed.

I was raised by a mother, and an older sister, who taught me domestic skills. I was proficient at cleaning, laundry, keeping a home, and cooking — Northern style cooking. One of my first humorous stories about the differences between those brought up in the north and those who call the south their home is about Pimento Cheese sandwiches (if you are Southern, yes, it's capitalized).

In my church circle of wonderful women who met monthly for fellowship, to study God's word and perform mission tasks, I was the only one who was retired. It came time to host a community luncheon during the Easter Lenten season and each circle was to provide fifty Pimento Cheese sandwiches for the event.

I was taken under the wing of the head kitchen lady who gave me specific instructions. The bread must be white sandwich bread, crusts cut off, and the finished sandwiches were to be cut on a diagonal. These culinary gems were then to be placed in a plastic container with a slightly damp paper towel covering them before the lid closed.

Following those specifics about the sandwich construction, I was given the recipe. Under no circumstances was I to purchase a premade cheese spread. By the time I had been told, step-by-step, what was expected, I was intimidated, and unsure of my capability. Me, the woman who had prepared and served full, complicated dinners for many people, now had shaking knees over the preparation of cheese-spread sandwiches.

The day before the event, I shopped and began the preparations. I hand-grated three pounds of cheddar cheese, opened and drained the pimentos, carefully measured the precise amount of Duke Mayonnaise, and folded the mixture together. Not ever having had Pimento Cheese before moving to South Carolina, I believed the mixture was passable.

I had just begun to spread the mixture onto the crust-less bread when my doorbell rang. It was Leslie, a member of the Circle. She had a container of premade Pimento Cheese, which she handed to me.

"I can't stay," she said. "I just wanted to drop this off so you'd be sure to have enough spread for the sandwiches."

I was dumbfounded and confused. "But, but," I stammered, "I thought we weren't allowed to use purchased spread."

Leslie laughed. "Are you kidding? We all do. Wish I could stay to help you but I've got a meeting. See you tomorrow."

I closed the door, carried the container of cheese to the kitchen, and wondered if I would ever figure out what was going on.

From that time on, the ladies in the church gathered around this newcomer and helped me understand that there was a Head-Church-Kitchen-Lady way, and there was their way. I learned about frozen biscuits, Jiffy cornbread mix, and all sorts of other shortcuts. Through these lessons I also learned to no longer be anxious about whether my cooking skills from the north would transfer to the south. They did just fine.

The southern recipe is: Sometimes…just go to the supermarket and get prepared mix!

HEAD CHURCH-KITCHEN LADY'S PIMENTO CHEESE SPREAD

Ingredients

1 pound sharp cheddar cheese, grated

1 2-ounce jar of diced (and drained) pimentos

¾ teaspoon dry mustard

fresh ground pepper to taste

3 tablespoons (or more) Duke's mayonnaise

Toni Armstrong Sample

19

SEASONED WITH SALT

Let your conversation be always full of grace, seasoned with salt,

so that you may know how to answer everyone.

Colossians 4:6 NIV

Frying pancakes reminds me of my seventh grade home economics class. I loved cooking, but often my cooking ended in flops. The egg yolks broke when I turned the fried eggs, and the toast burned. But the day we made cornmeal pancakes, I felt certain I had a winner. The pancakes were perfectly round and golden brown. I eagerly took the first bite — and spit it out. Too salty!

Alas, my teacher discovered my mistake when she sampled them. No top grades for me in this class. Sigh.

Fifty years later, with a master's degree in home economics, I made cornmeal pancakes again. They weren't perfectly round, but they weren't too salty. As I ate them with melted butter and maple syrup, I remembered my first salty ones and thought about being the salt of the earth. And I wondered, *Is it possible to be too salty?* Maybe I am when:

I'm pushy and preachy in sharing my faith.

I talk too much and don't listen.

I use complicated biblical words and assume others understand them.

In these instances, my interactions may have the same effect as my overly salted pancakes. They leave a bad taste.

But, more often, I am not salty enough. When opportunities to share my faith come, I say nothing. And sometimes my life doesn't look any different from those who don't know Jesus. Then I've lost my saltiness.

My life and actions will never be perfect, but with God's help, I want to be a good witness, reflect Jesus, and leave a good taste behind.

Heavenly Father, guide my conversation so it is always full of grace and seasoned with just the right amount of salt, that I may know how to answer everyone I talk to about Jesus. In Your name. Amen.

You are the salt of the earth.
But if the salt loses its saltiness, how can it be made salty again?
Matthew 5:13 NIV

CORNMEAL PANCAKES

Prepare this delicious recipe, or use the one for corn pancakes found on the box of Jiffy Corn Muffin Mix.

Ingredients

1 cup flour	2 eggs
1 cup yellow cornmeal	1⅓ cups milk
3 tablespoons sugar	2 tablespoons butter, melted
1 tablespoon baking powder	1 teaspoon vanilla
½ teaspoon salt	

Directions

1. Mix dry ingredients in a large bowl.
2. Mix liquid ingredients in a medium-sized bowl.
3. Add liquid ingredients to dry ingredients and mix until blended. Mixture may be slightly lumpy.
4. Fry in preheated skillet. Use oil, butter, or nonstick spray to prevent pancakes from sticking.
5. Pour ¼ cup pancake batter onto skillet for each 3- to 4-inch pancake.

6. When pancakes bubble and bottoms are golden brown, turn and cook until second side is golden brown.

Serve with butter and maple syrup. Or sweeten with honey or golden syrup (such as Lyle's brand; available in some grocery stores).
Makes about 16 pancakes.

Variations

Blueberry-Lemon Pancakes: Stir ¾ cup fresh blueberries or huckleberries and one teaspoon lemon zest into prepared batter.
Bacon Cornmeal Pancakes: Stir 4 to 6 cooked and crumbled bacon strips into prepared batter.
Corndog Pancakes: Cut little smokie hot dogs into thin circles. Place six slices on top of each pancake before turning to fry second side.

MAPLE-FLAVORED SYRUP

Ingredients

1 cup granulated sugar

1 cup brown sugar, firmly packed

1 cup water

½ teaspoon maple flavoring

Directions

1. Pour sugars and water into a saucepan.
2. Cook over medium heat until sugar dissolves and syrup comes to a boil, stirring frequently with a wooden spoon.
3. Boil syrup for 1 minute.
4. Remove from heat. Stir in maple flavoring.

Makes 1½ cups syrup.

Lydia E. Harris

20

A Christmas Whoops!

Proudly strutting round and round
Was a soon-to-be Christmas meal.
Little did that turkey know
How strange he soon would feel!

Time passed on and that turkey's strut
Led him right to a pan in the oven
To be enjoyed at dinner time
By moms and dads and cousins.

The moment arrived, the turkey was done,
All gathered round to stare
At how plump and stuffed the turkey was.
What a shock awaited us there.

The sight we saw was definitely not
A chest plumped up with bread!
We expected a Dolly Parton.
We got a Phyllis Diller instead.

This turkey was flat-chested
And much to our despair,
We couldn't find the stuffing
It really wasn't there.

Suddenly, we had the answer.
It caused the cooks to frown.
Would you believe we roasted
That poor turkey upside down!

With one big flip of that turkey
The meal was still a success.
But you can imagine the teasing
We cooks continue to get.

Juanita Giberson Woodward

21

CROWS AND RAVENS AND THE GOD OF ELIJAH

He struts across the grass in my front yard, his large size wrapped in a sleek black coat, sometimes revealing a glistening blue amid his feathers. In the crow family, crows and ravens are world famous as great workers for the "clean-up committee." The expression "something (or nothing) to crow about," or "he had to eat crow" is a description everyone understands.

They may not be our favorite birds, but God seems to have had regard for them. The Bible has several references to ravens and God enlisted their help to feed a prophet!

I watch from my kitchen window the crows spy the stale bread under my crape myrtle tree. They are vocal, loud, sneaky, viewed as greedy, territorial, certainly discerning, maybe "tribal." Not very lovable. Some do not share, but this morning, there is a difference. The first one perches on the top of the street lamp above the tree and surveys the area. Before long, a "cawing session" begins, "Hey, come see what I found!" When he gets no response, he flies away but returns later with the same shrill call, "Come! Here is a loaded table!"

The crackers in my cabinet were tasteless and old so I threw them out. One crow comes, picks up a cracker and using his beak for a bag, tromps off to the next door neighbor's yard. He bites off a small piece, drops it, then flies away, leaving the rest on the grass.

Was it tasteless or did he need a drink to be able to down it? I have seen them take pieces of bread to the birdbath.

He is soon back, searching. "Where is it? I know I left it here.

Ahh, here it is." One more bite on the hard crust and it is downed.

He flies to the top of the lamp post cawing, interpreted as, "This is something new, come grab a bite!" Others join him. The crackers are quickly devoured.

Crows are smart. God has given intelligence to all of his creation. One returns the next morning, does a survey, finds nothing, flies away. No ad for crow country that day, but a great reminder for me: I can tell people where to find the Bread of Life that satisfies.

While I feed birds, birds have never fed me. However, an almost humorous event has been injected in the very serious narrative of 1 Kings 17, 18 telling us how God used ravens to feed Elijah the prophet. Elijah had been given the responsibility to tell the great king Ahab that judgment in the form of a famine was about to fall on Israel. There would be neither dew nor rain in the coming days except by Elijah's command. No crops, no food. Hunger is a compelling influence.*

Ahab was idolatrous, wicked to the core. Everything had been going along so well the people had ignored God. Why should Ahab or the people believe Elijah? God knew Ahab would retaliate. God prepared and protected Elijah by telling him to make a fast getaway and hide himself by a small brook. There, God commanded ravens to bring bread and meat twice a day. Elijah had to trust God and accept his provision or starve to death. He survived and confronted Ahab, not without some fear. Read the story and discover how God kept his promise and the rain did come.

Amos the sheepherder also prophesied a famine to come — not for food, but for hearing the Word of God. Could that be today? Jesus said he is the Bread and Water of Life, but many people have not partaken of his feast. Are Christians willing to "caw" and invite people to the table set by our Lord — to see that others are fed and watered so they do not die eternally? Are we willing to "crow" about this?

*Several famines are mentioned in the Old Testament: 1 Kings

17–18; 2 Kings 6:18, 8:1; Amos 8:11; John 6:35; John 4:21.

I am not much of a cook, but there are some things I do like to use when I have special guests.

Myrtle V. Thompson

CURRY DIP

Myrtle V. Thompson

Ingredients

1½ cups of Hellman's Light mayo

2 teaspoons curry powder

1 tablespoon finely minced onion

2 teaspoons French's Mustard

Directions

1. Mix ingredients together.
2. Serve with veggies or on crackers.

(I have added it to Chicken salad.)

MOM'S TASTIES

Mom made her own biscuit dough but the commercial kind can be used.

Ingredients

Biscuits
Sausage

Directions

1. Break up sausage into small bits and fry lightly.
2. Drain on a paper towel.
3. Roll out each of the biscuits into an oblong piece (using two is easier, makes a larger roll).
4. Place sausage pieces on the dough and roll like a jellyroll.
5. Bake at temperature suggested on the biscuit container.
6. Serve warm.

22

GIANT COOKIE CAPER

My children did not realize that you could bake cookies from "scratch." They believed that homemade cookies only came out of tubes that I bought at the store. There are reasons they believed this way. I call it the "giant cookie caper."

The four years my husband was in Bible College I worked to help support his education and we put off having children. After his graduation, we immediately accepted a senior pastorate at a small rural church.

For so many wives in the ministry, everyone assumes you are naturally a great cook. But, because I had not had children until six years after we were married and I had worked full time those six years, our meals had been hurried affairs that I put together after a long day on the job. Cooking and baking had been completely out.

And because I had been raised my entire life in the city, the rural environment was hard for me to get used to. I quickly realized that all these wives of ranchers and farmers were wonderful cooks, bakers and managers of time. I came to see that this was a learning season for me in the area of cooking and baking and time management.

When our son was born, it was a new adventure for me as a mother. Since I had never even experienced babysitting, motherhood was a challenge. I got lots of help and suggestions from women in our churches that helped me gain confidence in child rearing. However, I still never learned to bake, especially cookies.

When our son was five, we adopted our daughter who was three weeks old. Our son was thrilled to have a new baby sister and I again entered the world of raising a baby. As our children grew, I tried to learn to bake things for them, but cooking and baking was not as easy as it looked. I got advice from both my mother and mother-in-law but when it came to cookies, I was lost.

My children were still quite young when I decided one day to bake cookies from scratch for them. I vividly remember the incident. It began when I asked myself, *"How hard can it be to make cookies?"*

My children, eager to finally have some homemade cookies, watched me the entire time. They always had store bought ones up until this time.

I got out my favorite Betty Crocker Cookbook and all the ingredients for chocolate chip cookies then began to mix the dough. As I mixed it I thought it didn't look right so began adding things not called for in the recipe. I finally had a bowl of dough that I thought looked just right, so I dropped spoonsful of it onto the cookie sheet.

I checked the oven temperature, waited till it pre-heated and then carefully placed my beloved cookies in the oven. Anxiously we all waited the few minutes until my timer told us they were done. I reached in the oven and took out a pan of cookies…that was one giant cookie. I had put the spoonsful of dough too close together.

My children looked at me in amazement and with raised eyebrows and wanted to know what happened. Of course I couldn't tell them that I had "altered" the recipe so I smiled and said, "They are perfect." Both looked skeptical until I said, "I made a cookie for a giant."

We had a good laugh over that and then I carefully cut our giant cookie into small squares like I would do for brownies. Although they were a little doughy and thick, my kids thought they were great.

After this fiasco I realized that I just was not a baker. I tried a few more times but it was always the same. I asked myself why, if I could make a lemon pie couldn't I make cookies?

As my children grew, I was asked to bring "treats" to their schools or club meetings. I was always willing to bring something "special" because it was store bought. All the other mothers would bring home baked goods, but my children thought I was special because I always brought store bought items, at least I had convinced them of this.

My children are now grown and my daughter is a wonderful cook. Where she got her ability I still question. I am amazed when she produces outstanding meals. She can whip up cupcakes and cookies without any effort. Our son, after he was married, also began to cook and now cooks often although he, too, is not a baker.

So if you feel you are a terrible mom for not baking for your kids, remember there are those of us out there who still can't bake a cookie but can give the gift of encouragement to others and share how we lived through a humorous experience.

Beverly Hill McKinney

23

RECIPES, RISK, AND RICE KRISPIE TREATS

My brother and I had what pediatricians refer to as "unadventurous palettes" when we were young. We were picky to the point we rejected normal foods. We didn't like oatmeal. Or ham. Or even sandwiches.

And then we grew up. Our palettes matured. We started cooking for ourselves.

My brother is good in the kitchen. So am I. And we're both adventurous, each of us according to our own design. His cooks by intuition, opening the cupboard and transforming whatever he finds into something delicious. I rely on recipe books, perusing them to discover something interesting to try. His is art and mine, I suppose, is science.

We live in different states now, but because we spend a week together at Fishtrap Lake in Minnesota every summer, I've learned that his Rice Krispie Treats are better than mine. Much better. If it wasn't for him, my kids wouldn't even know that those staples of childhood could originate from a kitchen because the ones at our house come wrapped in cellophane. My brother looked at a pile of marshmallows, butter, and Rice Krispies and knew that more marshmallows would make a better bar. I followed the recipe and ended up with something dry and undesirable. Both his way and mine carry risks and potential for failure. He trusts his instincts.

A couple of summers back I went to the library and checked out a little cookbook filled with all kinds of interesting recipes for dips and sauces. The one for curried hummus caught my attention. While I'm not fond of hummus, I do like curry, and I wondered if curry might build a culinary bridge. This would, I decided, be something to take to the lake. I bought the ingredients my pantry lacked, whirled them together in the food processor, scooped the results onto a cracker, and popped it into the mouth of the first person to pass through the kitchen — my husband.

In an unusual display of drama, he lit around the kitchen like a scorched cat suddenly overcome by a hairball. "What is that?" he spat, his look communicating that I had lost not only my mind, but possibly my kitchen rights along with it. I wasn't sure what his problem was. I had tried it. It wasn't that bad. It wasn't that good, either. Curry had not built a bridge.

Undeterred, I packed it in the cooler, hoping the rest of the family would react differently, especially my culinarily-adventurous, globe-trotting brother.

My husband explained in detail the awfulness of the hummus as I was setting it out for a mid-afternoon snack.

My brother quietly mentioned that he didn't really like curry, but he picked up a cracker, scooped up some hummus, and put it into his mouth. Silence settled over the room as he chewed. He swallowed. He broke the silence when, with a restrained expression said, "Nice try." He patted me on the head as if to say, "Never do that again," and escaped the cabin to go fishing.

No one else even tried the hummus.

I'm looking for something new, probably something less interesting, to take to the lake this summer. Whatever it is, it might be fabulous. Or a complete failure. Either way, I know we'll have my brother's Rice Krispie Treats to fall back on.

Natalie Ogbourn

CURRY HUMMUS FOR THE BRAVE

Natalie Ogbourne

Ingredients

2 15-ounce cans chickpeas, rinsed and drained

4 tablespoons olive oil

2 -3 garlic cloves, to taste

3 teaspoons curry

1 teaspoon cumin

4 tablespoons lemon juice

salt, to taste

Directions

1. Place all ingredients in food processor bowl and blend until smooth.

2. Transfer to serving bowl.

3. Drizzle with olive oil, if desired.

Serve with pita chips, cut raw veggies, or crackers.

24

AN ACCEPTABLE STIR-FRY

In the days before cell phones, my husband Sean went grocery shopping for items to feed his parents when they traveled from California to visit us in Indiana. With the menus — and grocery list — chiseled in stone, he had to improvise when the cabbage was sold out.

No problem.

A nearby bin held heaps of red cabbage with its distinctive and beautiful red-purple coloring.

Upon Sean's arrival at home, we discussed the vivid cabbage and that I had never used anything but green. We concluded that it tastes the same.

No problem.

Might even cook up prettier than the green cabbage.

Later that day, my new in-laws arrived. All went well *until* I began the supper preparations.

We lived in an apartment above my grandmother, so I set up in her bigger kitchen. I declined all offers of help, so my new relatives could visit with my oldest relative.

While conversation drifted into the kitchen, I pulled the chicken breasts from the oven, deboned them, and cut them into the most perfect cubes I could fashion. I really wanted to impress Larry and Joni.

I sliced green peppers into strips and diced onions into a tidy pile. The carrots came as close to uniform little orange discs as I could manage. Visions of the perfect stir-fry filled my head. What a pretty contrast these carrots would make with the purple cabbage.

Cabbage! I quickly set to work sawing the leaves into narrow ribbons.

When the oil sizzled in the wok, I began adding ingredients.

Carrots and cabbage came first as they took the longest to cook.

As I stirred, the first hint of trouble appeared. My colorful, high-contrast veggies were fading.

No problem.

Well, maybe a little problem because the carrots were turning an orangey, purple color I had never seen before.

After a brief what-will-my-in-laws-think panic, I assured myself the meal would be fine once I added the other ingredients.

Next, I mixed in the cooked chicken to re-warm. Warm it did, and morphed into cubes of a lovely shade of lavender.

Uh-oh. I definitely have a problem.

Positioning myself where no one else in the living room could see me, I waved Sean into the kitchen for a consult. Pointing to the content of the wok, I asked, "What do I? What do *we* do now?"

What could we do? No way to deny I had been cooking their evening meal. No money to take them out to eat instead.

We sampled the psychedelic purple mishmash.

Sean shrugged. "Tastes like stir-fry."

So we stirred in the peppers and onion and watched that purple cabbage's influence take hold. The onions turned an unappealing purple-gray and the green peppers turned...not green.

I stared at my rainbow of purple hues. "I wanted to make an impression on your parents."

Sean placed the soy sauce on the table. "You're definitely going to make an impression."

We debated just serving the food or warning them. We went with the warning. But it's hard to prepare yourself for something you've never seen before.

We all gathered around the table in the kitchen. Then, after staring at my creation for some prolonged moments, Larry spoke what I've come to recognize as his signature anticipatory line.

"Oh my goodness!" He grabbed the soy sauce, sprinkled some onto the unusual mess on his plate, and took a bite.

The tension broken, we laughed. The laughter continued throughout the meal — one we would never forget.

I had hoped to make an impression on Sean's parents, but they made a lasting impression on me. The acceptance I felt that night from my new in-laws has continued through almost thirty years of marriage.

And, my father-in-law for years asserted, "That was the best purple stir-fry I ever tasted."

Kim Peterson

SIMPLE STIR-FRY

Kim Peterson

Ingredients

2 chicken breasts
1 green cabbage
3 carrots
1 white onion
½ green pepper
¼ cup peanut oil
(substitution: vegetable or canola oil)

20-25 snow pea pods
(substitution: sugar snap pea pods.)

½ cup bean sprouts
(optional)

Low-sodium soy sauce

Make Ahead

1. Bake the two chicken breasts.

2. While warm, remove skin and debone.

3. Chop into cubes or tear into bite-size shreds.

Meal-time Preparation

1. Green cabbage - Slice into ribbons ½-inch wide and 3 inches long.

2. Carrots - Peel and slice into thin circles. For larger carrots, cut the slices into half moons.

3. White onion - Peel and cut into eighths. Separate the slices.

4. Green pepper - Cut into narrow strips. Use more if you prefer a stronger green pepper flavor.

Directions

1. Heat oil in wok or cast iron skillet.

2. When hot, add carrot slices.

3. Cook 3-4 minutes then add the ribbons of cabbage.

4. Stir well to coat the cabbage in the oil.

5. Keep the oil hot enough to cook quickly without burning the vegetables.

6. Once cabbage softens, add the onion and green pepper, stirring frequently.

7. When all the vegetables are cooked to the desired texture, toss in the snow pea pods and bean sprouts cooking only long enough to heat them, retaining their crispiness.

Serving Ideas

At the table, sprinkle on low-sodium soy sauce to taste. Pair with egg rolls and duck sauce to complete the meal.

Variation

For a different stir-fry, substitute a sliced rope of Polska Kielbasa for the chicken. Omit the soy sauce and bean sprouts, and add slices of yellow summer squash and zucchini.

DUCK SAUCE FOR EGG ROLLS

Ingredients

½ jar apricot jam
(substitution: seedless
black raspberry or plum)

apple cider vinegar to taste

Directions

1. In a non-stick saucepan, melt the jam or jelly on low to medium heat.

2. Stir in apple cider vinegar a tablespoon at a time until desired sweet-sour flavor is achieved.

Serves 4 to 6.

25

SOLID AS A ROCK

Growing up, my brother, sister and I looked forward to when Daddy cooked. Our favorites were his sausage gravy and biscuits, or chicken and dumplings. We got those on the rare occasions when Mama was out of town.

Daddy would pull out a thin green cookbook he and Mama received as a wedding present years before any of us were born. From there he would mix up and make homemade biscuits or dumplings. They were scrumptious and so flaky that they would melt in your mouth.

After I got married, I wanted to surprise my husband with Daddy's homemade biscuits. I didn't have a copy of his recipe, but decided to try to recreate the biscuits from memory. Why I didn't call and ask for the recipe, I'll never know, other than I was too obstinate.

I mixed the ingredients and popped them into the oven, then took them out and arranged them in a basket and proudly set them in front of my new husband, although they didn't quite look like the beautiful, flaky biscuits I remembered Daddy making.

"Um, thanks," he mumbled, trying to get the words out between bites. "What did you do?" He knocked the biscuit on the table but it remained solid as a rock. We couldn't pry them apart even with a knife.

Deciding those biscuits were for the birds, we took them out back. Throwing them against the back of the carport did not make them break. We started laughing as we threw them. I'd completely goofed, and nothing was going to break them.

That became a conversation piece about how much of a cook I wasn't. On more than one occasion the reminder of this experience kept me from cooking duties.

However, cooking is like our faith. We can keep making

mistakes and never learn from them or we can learn until our faith is unbreakable.

Psalm 18:2 NLT tells us: *The LORD is my rock, my fortress, and my savior; my God is my rock, in whom I find protection.*

When we're up against opposition and feel we have nowhere to turn, there is one who is always there for us.

Although my husband likes to be able to bite into and chew what I've cooked, God wants our faith to be like those biscuits. So strong that nothing will break them.

He is our rock. We can always turn to him.

Diana Leagh Matthews

26

DELIGHT COMES IN LAYERS

I used to be amazed at the number of Christian writers and bloggers putting their stories out through traditional publishing or by self-publishing books, blogs, or vlogs. After personal computers became affordable, the masses instantly had a "voice" and became writers and speakers. But weren't there enough people preaching and teaching the Gospel? Would it really make a difference to have one more person out there in the world quoting scripture and conversing about theologians' commentary?

The answer popped into my head immediately: God meets every individual in a different place because every individual was created unique, therefore, various stories and recapped experiences are needed. And because individuals have different interests and varied stories to tell, the more the Gospel is shared along with personal testimonies, the greater the odds are that one of those stories will register with a nonbeliever or an agnostic who might be "riding the fence" of their salvation. Another person's testimony could possibly help usher an unbeliever into the throne room of grace.

I may never know how much my testimony has impacted others or how effective my efforts have been until I get to heaven. But I can hope that once I'm home, God will share the results with me and tell me whether or not my efforts were effective; if he was delighted with the fruit of my labor; and if my outreach to others for him made progress my eyes couldn't see.

I knew this much, God had delighted me with many gifts and treasured moments before I ever thought about trying to delight him in return with the meager and limited resources I own here on earth.

I realized something about God and a word He'd used: *delight*.

My earthly father loved delighting me when he was alive — especially during the holidays when celebrating the birthday of Jesus. But my heavenly Father loves delighting me more. God's gifts, if I'm paying attention, are seen as layered delight throughout a lifetime of walking with Him.

Yes, God has always delighted in giving his children good gifts. Matthew 7:11 tells us: *If you then, being evil, know how to give good gifts to your children, how much more will your Father who is in heaven give what is good to those who ask Him! In everything, then, do to others as you would have them do to you. For this is the essence of the Law and the Prophets.* (Author's paraphrase)

These days, my all-time favorite verse about the word *delight* is this: *Delight yourself in the Lord; and He will give you the desires of your heart.* (Psalm 37:4 ESV) There have been numerous times this verse resonated with me.

But how can I ever delight the Lord back with a gift of my own? He's the One who created the Universe and owns all the cattle on a thousand hills. How can I possibly give him any earthly thing that will please him? Delighting my earthly father was easy in comparison. When Daddy was still with me, all I had to do to please him was to prepare his favorite dessert, Four Layer Delight, and he was happy for days.

But what to give my heavenly Father — the God who has everything — to delight Him? There was and still is one recipe: I am to give him *all* of me, just as he gave his One and Only Son for the entire world. Through the gift of his Son, I was assured of redemption and the way back to him for eternal life. It is as hard and as simple as that once the life changing steps are taken.

Once the messiness of surrendering all has been laid out, wrapped up and tied with a bow, other ways to delight God will come — the fruit of labor in his service will be produced as a sweet sacrifice — though one can never outdo God in gift giving or in trying to delight him. He's always been and will always be the best gift giver ever — showering his children throughout a lifetime of love layers embedded with delightful gifts, even during the hard times sure to come.

I've shared the recipe with the ingredients to make my heavenly Father happy, now I'll share the ingredients to a recipe that made my earthly father happy until time for him to leave this world and return home. I hope it delights your loved ones as much as it does mine.

Vicki H. Moss

Four Layer Delight

Vicki H. Moss

Ingredients

1 stick of butter or margarine, softened

1 cup flour

½ cup finely chopped pecans

1 8-ounce package cream cheese, softened

1 large carton of Cool Whip

1 cup powdered confectioner's sugar, sifted

2 packages of instant chocolate pudding and pie mix

3 cups milk

Directions

Preheat oven to 350°.

1st layer –Mix softened butter or margarine, flour, and pecans. Spread in a square pan (Pyrex dish is good) and bake for 10 min. at 350°.

2nd layer – Cream softened cream cheese. Add 1 cup of Cool Whip plus 1 tablespoon of milk and the sifted powdered sugar. Mix together and spread over the first layer.

3rd layer – Mix the powdered chocolate pudding with the milk. Pour over other layers.

4th layer – Spread rest of Cool Whip over pudding. Garnish by sprinkling toasted pecans on top if so desired.

Refrigerate to let the layers set up.

27

CLOVES ARE GROUND?

Cooking has never been my strength. I grew up watching my amazing, Kansas-born-and-bred mother cook for the five of us, fixing three basic yet varied and substantial meals complete with a delicious dessert, practically every day. It exhausts me to think of all she did.

Contemplating the effort that went into preparing the meats and the vegetables, the potatoes and the salads, the pies and cakes and puddings that graced our groaning kitchen table every single day astonishes me. All this without a microwave and the convenience of frozen food. On top of that, we had both milk and water at the evening meal, and afterward my hard-working mother washed every single dish, utensil, glass, and pan by hand.

As a child growing up in the typical mid-western community of Webster Groves, a suburb of St. Louis, I wasn't asked to do a lot of chores, but I remember one rather insignificant task. Following the dinner meal, my responsibility was to towel dry our everyday silverware, actual sterling silver, along with the pots and pans. Since there was often something else I wanted to do, like ride my bike or play with the neighbors, I admit my attitude wasn't always the best.

Over time, I began to understand the labor involved in preparing our meals and began washing the dishes to help, but that was not a regular pattern. Occasionally, my mother got a break from cooking when our family ate dinner at the local Steak 'n Shake. Truly, a lot of cooking, and a lot of sacrifice, was what mothers did back then, and any respite was welcomed.

Those "back then" wonder years spanned the post-World War II era of the 1950s and 1960s, when mothers mostly worked inside the home. They prepared meals and took care of their household, while their Baby-Boomer children planned for college. Going to college was expected in my family. A degree was necessary, my parents said, in case I needed to have my own livelihood. Plus, I come from a line of college-educated women. Remarkably, my mother received her B.S. in Physical Education in 1932 from what is now Kansas State University in Manhattan, where her father was head of the math department. Her mother, my grandmother, even more astonishingly earned her degree in 1897 from the same school, known then as Kansas State Agricultural College.

Thus, I was encouraged to study and participate, and I did. There were high school activities that included drama and the yearbook staff to hone responsibility, church choir and youth fellowship to grow my knowledge and faith in God, and the YMCA for developing confident leadership skills. In addition, there was Girl Scouts for learning about and enjoying the outdoors, earning merit badges, and doing service projects. Finally, there was the satisfaction of volunteering over 100 hours as a Candy Striper at Barnes Hospital in St. Louis, just two bus rides from our home.

Cooking didn't fit into this busy schedule. My mother was preparing slaw once, and while munching on a cabbage leaf, I asked in all innocence how I would know the difference between cabbage and lettuce. She smiled and said I'd know when the time came.

Indeed, the time did come. In August of 1967 I married my late first husband, Arie. In September, I started my sophomore year at Bradley University in Peoria, Illinois, as a new bride majoring in elementary education. I eagerly embraced being both a student and a wife. Since I grew up watching my mother model a commitment to domestic responsibilities that encompassed cooking, cleaning, laundry, ironing, and sewing, I began married life with a similar commitment. While I understood the basics of each task and could manage them, cooking would require more on-the-job training to increase my confidence in that area.

In the pre-computer age, cookbooks were especially valuable and appropriate as wedding gifts, and those I received became the foundation of my collection. I started as a culinary neophyte and had many challenges, but Christmas, 1967, is still the occasion of my most humiliating cooking blunder.

Inexperience, ignorance, well, chalk it up to being a newlywed, but the embarrassment has never been forgotten. The normal holiday excitement took on added meaning that year, as I planned to bake special gifts to give to new family, friends, and my husband's boss, Mr. Everett Mooberry. He was the principal at McKinley School in Peoria, where Arie worked as a Home Counselor.

One of the books I had received is titled *Favorite Recipes of Missouri, Family Edition.* I turned to the Quick Breads section for an easy yet delicious gift choice, and the Pumpkin Bread seemed perfect. I looked over the recipe and made my grocery list, including a can of pumpkin and a box of raisins. Cinnamon and cloves were already on the pantry shelf.

Christmas Break was nearing when I gathered up the ingredients and greased the three loaf pans required. I mixed the eggs, sugar, shortening and pumpkin, and then measured the dry ingredients into another bowl. The cinnamon was added without hesitation, but when I picked up the small tin of cloves, a thought skittered through my mind. Will these work? Well, since they were cloves and that's what the recipe called for, sure, and into the bowl went my awkward one-half teaspoonful of whole cloves.

After the bread cooled, I wrapped the loaves in plastic and added colorful bows. The first gift was for Mr. Mooberry and his wife. I looked it over carefully before Arie left for work, happy to bear my efforts. While I saw a few whole cloves nestled comfortably in the rounded top, I never felt any concern. I guess Arie didn't either. Cloves were cloves, right?

There is a very old, original idiom, from 1605 actually, that applies to my story: *The proof of the pudding is in the eating* (word-detective.com). The bread looked so yummy, I decided we could eat one of the loaves, and I'd make more later. I prepared a slice to have with my second cup of coffee and studied it with satisfaction, a lovely pumpkin orange shaded with cinnamon, with dark raisins and several whole cloves winking up at me. Hmm. Was I supposed to use whole cloves? But how else did they come?

One hard bite confirmed my fears, and I hurried to Kroger's to see what I could find out. Since this was the pre-home computer, pre-Google, and pre-Siri era, I couldn't just type or ask a question and receive an answer. Instead, it required time, effort and gasoline to get a resolution

At last I scurried down the baking aisle and found shelves of spices, and there they were: tins of Ground Cloves tucked in next to the Whole Cloves. I had never noticed.

Did Mr. Mooberry and his wife laugh and throw their gift away when they saw it? I never heard, gracious as they were, but they probably did. After all, I threw mine out. I never made pumpkin bread again without recalling my mistake and how easy it is to make a culinary blunder, especially as a cooking novice!

Ann Brubaker Greenleaf Wirtz

28

SIMPLE IS BEST

Although I love baking, I rarely do it. For most of the year, my mixing bowl and measuring spoons go unused thanks to my busy schedule.

When Christmastime arrived one year, my stomach did a cartwheel. Finally, I'd tie my apron around my waist and have some fun in the kitchen. No work calls or emails would distract me.

Scrolling the internet for recipes, I found two that stood out — one for butter cookies and one for gingerbread cookies. Both looked extremely detailed, and I was ready for a challenge.

Then I remembered a batch of spice cookies that a lady from church had brought to a women's gathering. The recipe she shared was simple, but I remembered the soft morsels that tasted of cinnamon and nutmeg. So, I added the ingredients to my shopping list.

In my kitchen — with "Silent Night" playing in the background — I started mixing the dough for the gingerbread cookies. The list of ingredients was almost a page long, and many needed to be mixed together separately. The butter cookies were the same way — taking nearly an hour to blend before going into the oven.

The spice cookies were quite the opposite. Following the recipe, I plopped three ingredients into a bowl, then placed spoonsful of dough on a tray and slid it into the oven. Only fifteen minutes spent, and I had a perfect batch of round confections.

On Christmas day at my parents' house, my mom and dad enjoyed all three varieties.

"But which is your *favorite*?" I asked.

Both pointed to the spice cookies.

"Really?" I chuckled. "Those were the easy ones."

Later at my in-laws, the spice cookies were once again the

favorite. I grinned, knowing how quick they'd been to make.

I'm reminded of the story of Mary and Martha, two sisters who knew and loved Jesus. One day when the Lord stopped at their home, Mary sat at his feet and listened to his words, while Martha worked on "preparations that had to be made."

Martha, upset that her sister wasn't lending a hand, asked Jesus to intervene. *"Martha, Martha," the Lord answered, "you are worried and upset about many things, but few things are needed — or indeed only one. Mary has chosen what is better, and it will not be taken away from her"* (Luke 10:41-42 NIV).

Next Christmas, I want to spend more time celebrating Jesus with my loved ones. I want to sit at their feet, listening to how their lives are going. I want to trade stories and let our laughter light up the room.

To make time, I'll stick with the easy spice cookies, nothing else. They taste better, anyway.

SPICE COOKIES

Ingredients:

1 box spice cake mix

⅓ cup vegetable oil

2 eggs

Optional: ¾ cups raisins or nuts

Directions:

Preheat oven to 350°.

1. Line cookie sheet(s) with parchment paper.

2. Combine ingredients in bowl and mix well.

3. Drop by heaping tablespoons on parchment paper.

4. Bake in oven for 10-12 minutes.

Lauren Craft

29

DON'T POSTPONE JOY

Martha had enough. Her sister Mary did it again, left her to do all the work while she just sat there. Martha was distracted by all the preparations. And though the very source of Joy was with her, she was focused on what she had to do.

Sound familiar?

But the Lord answered and said to her, *"Martha, Martha, you are worried and bothered about so many things; but only one thing is necessary, for Mary has chosen the good part, which shall not be taken away from her."* (Luke 10:41-42 NASB)

But how can life really be about one thing? Without Martha, no food would have been served.

On a slow morning, sitting on a dock facing the intracoastal waterway in Wilmington, North Carolina, I'm once again pondering how to be a Mary without neglecting my responsibilities.

The mid-morning sun warms the steady breeze as it massages my face. I look across the gray blue waterway and see white caps ushering the tide to my right. The rhythmic waves lap upon the shore interrupted only by the rubbing of the floating docks along the pile-driven wooden poles, the squawking of sea birds and the distant sound of a dog's bark.

I have sought my own answers to this quandary for years, but this morning it all seems clear. No profound answers are given, only his strong hand outstretched; inviting me to give him my concerns, so I can be with him. Together, he will show me how to live a Mary life in a Martha world.

My cares are safely sealed, waiting for his commands to be revealed.

Two light yellow butterflies dart across the rolling tide. Above the water flow, there is a lime green strip of land below a line of emerald trees, couching white, multi-storied buildings in the distance. Above the tree line, a cloudless sky rises in deeper shades of pastel blue toward the heavens.

Wow! This is joy, this trusting, this resting, this enjoying his presence. Is this abiding? Is this what Jesus means when he tells me to remain in his love?

So, what now? I could regret millions of distracted moments in my past when I labored without a thought of his nearness.

But I won't.

I will go forth with a deeper understanding of what Jesus means when he tells me not to worry, but to seek his business, his Kingdom, his supremacy in my life.

All that other stuff, the things I seem to focus on, what I'll eat and what I'll wear and what I'll drink — he's got that. He and I have more important things to do, like enjoying this moment together.

And by the way, when I am doing that (enjoying moments of life with him) I will naturally love the people I meet along the way. When, like Mary, I'm in tune with my Lord's nearness, when I'm yielding to his Indwelling Spirit, his love flows through me to others. My number one concern now is to love others as he has loved me. This starts with resting in his love.

Jesus said, *"If you keep My commandments, you will abide in My love; just as I have kept My Father's commandments and abide in His love. These things I have spoken to you so that My joy may be in you, and that your joy may be made full. This is My commandment, that you love one another, just as I have loved you."* (John 15:10-12 NASB)

"Love is the overflow of joy in God that gladly meets the needs of others." (John Piper, *Desiring God*, p. 206)

In his presence is fullness of joy. (Psalm 16:11)

Whatever you eat or drink, or whatever you do,
you must do all for the glory of God.

1 Corinthians 10:31(NLT)

Rob Buck

30
THE GREAT TURKEY MISTAKE

I could smell the fragrance of the Scotch Pine Christmas tree and catch a whiff of the turkey baking in all the fragrant spices. The house was festive, decorated with everything I owned for the holidays. The crackling fire made everything so inviting.

My parents were coming and I was preparing my first Christmas dinner without my mother having to lift a finger. We had also invited an officer who was unable to make it home for the holiday and whom I secretly hoped to impress. Daddy had a special place in his heart for that local Air Force base since he met my mother there in 1945 during World War II.

As usual after Mom and Dad arrived, Mom wanted to help in the kitchen. It was not in her nature to sit around while food was being prepared. However, three hours earlier, I had washed the turkey, mixed spices to rub over the skin, basted it with butter, tied the legs together with string and confidently put the bird into the oven.

As I unwrapped the foil from the turkey that smelled and looked *so* good, I noticed my mother's eyes get as wide as saucers. I couldn't understand why. Mom leaned over and whispered, "You didn't take the gizzard out."

I said, "What gizzard?"

She gently explained that giblets are the internal organs of the turkey including the neck, liver, heart and gizzard of the bird. Some cooks use the giblets in gravy or stuffing but I was supposed to remove the gizzard before cooking the turkey.

A corner of paper sticking out of the turkey cavity was a clue that it was still in there. I was horrified. The last thing I wanted to see on Christmas was the gizzard of a turkey. Not then, not now, not ever! After seeing the shock on my face, my mother in her infinite wisdom, told me not to worry, that we would be able to salvage the turkey and ultimately the whole dinner.

She took out the giblets that were still wrapped in a burned paper bag and proceeded to carefully cut the meat off the bones, avoiding getting too close to the turkey cavity. Mom carved until she thought every safe piece of meat was on the platter. Meanwhile, I was almost sickened by the thought of disappointing my mom and making such a ghastly mistake on such a special day.

Mom set the seasoned turkey slices as the centerpiece of the table. Around the turkey platter I very carefully arranged the dishes of glazed baby carrots, green beans with crumbled bacon, southern style cornbread dressing, homemade buttermilk biscuits and a green salad dressed with sherry vinegar. Still-warm apple and cherry pies waited on the sideboard to be topped with vanilla ice cream and served for dessert. Everything looked and smelled mouth-watering. When Daddy said the blessing, I said a silent prayer hoping that disgusting gizzard had not somehow ruined the turkey.

Fortunately, the rest of the dinner came off without a hitch. The turkey was moist, tender, and absolutely delicious. I think my father knew something was up when he didn't get to carve the turkey at the table but he didn't say a word.

I'm not sure why I didn't think about it before the humiliation but I later realized that I had never seen my mother cook a whole turkey before! How was I supposed to know there was a surprise inside?

Thankfully the turkey was salvaged and nobody else was the wiser. After my parents went home, my mother told my father what had happened. Mom said all he did was shake his head.

And our special guest, the Air Force officer, kept complimenting me on the meal. I guess I did impress him because we started seeing each other a lot after that. And no, he never found out about my catastrophe in the kitchen that day.

The now legendary Christmas dinner turkey fiasco has been the running family joke every year when we all decide on the holiday menu and who is bringing what.

Since then, I have learned that it's okay to eat gizzards and they might even be tasty. However, I don't intend to eat either gizzards or the paper they come in.

I have to admit I have never cooked another whole turkey since that time almost 30 years ago. Instead I prefer to cook a turkey breast.

And I smile every time I put it in the oven.

AimeeAnn Blythe

31

PROOF OF THE PUDDING

"The proof of the pudding is in the eating," Miguel Cervantes wrote in *Don Quixote*. I believe that to be absolutely true, literally, not just figuratively!

"I don't eat pudding in any way, shape or form," my husband Ken had warned me when he spotted the package of banana pudding mix I'd set on the kitchen counter.

"I thought I'd mash up these two elderly bananas and stir them into the mix. I know you like banana cream pie."

"Make some banana bread instead. I don't do pudding."

Yes, Ken had definite do's and don'ts about what he'd eat. So now I added pudding to the mental list that already included lima beans, candied sweet potatoes and deviled eggs. When we first got married I'd been amusedly puzzled that he'd refused to sample some of the down home dishes Grandma had taught me to cook and that I dearly loved.

How could he be so fussy? After all, here was a fellow who bragged he'd savored snails in garlic sauce purchased from a street vendor a block from the Eiffel Tower, and lamented that Walmart didn't carry quark, a kind of yogurt cheese he bought when he lived in Germany.

But now, a few years into our late-in-life marriage, I began to be a bit troubled. I'd found myself more than once forced to toss out a dish that simply didn't please his palate. Ken knew how much I hated to throw any food away. My years in the Peace Corps had taught me "waste not, want not" when it came to edibles. Why, one spring as we weeded the front yard, I'd even mentioned I wished I could remember how Grandma had prepared what she called "a mess o' greens."

"I know she wilted the dandelion leaves in bacon grease, and added onion and garlic," I began, dreamily recalling the delicious aroma. "I think she added a dash of vinegar. Or maybe it was pepper sauce."

"It would be a mess, all right," Ken had retorted, yanking the weeds from my hand and tossing them into the wheelbarrow.

I usually went along with his preferences, but when it came to bread, I drew the line. I believed that letting bread grow stale or moldy amounted to blasphemy. Bread, I'd learned from Grandma, was the staff of life. Every crumb needed to be consumed.

So when ours started to stale I'd make croutons to sprinkle on French onion soup, crumbs to pad out meat loaf, or cubes to stir into stewed tomatoes. Then finally one day I noticed that some of the apples from our trees that I'd stored in our pantry last autumn had begun to look a bit dehydrated. We also had half a loaf of more-than-a-day-old French bread.

I thumbed through my recipe box and found Grandma's recipe for apple bread pudding. *Aha!* I told myself, ready to delve into a little deception. I'd have to call it something else. Maybe I'd claim it was Brown Betty. Grandma had made that, too, but it didn't contain milk and eggs. Ken wouldn't know the difference.

I headed for the kitchen to whip up dessert.

Sometimes Grandma served this with a sauce, either vanilla or caramel, but since Ken scrunched up his face at syrupy sauces, I'd simply top it with whipped cream, which he loved.

"Ready for dessert? I baked something this afternoon that I think you'll love."

Ken favored me with his lopsided smile. "What's it called?"

I averted my face as I scooped out a couple of servings into custard cups. I had a hard time telling even a little white lie without turning crimson. I squirted a little whipped cream as I thought about how to answer.

"Oh, it's just something Grandma used to bake," I said, carefully evading the question. "It's kind of an old fashioned dish, sort of like a Brown Betty with apples."

Ken ate every bite. "It's paradisiacal," he said. "I'll take a second helping. What all goes into it?"

I bit my lip. I didn't want to fib outright, so I handed him Grandma's recipe card.

"Bread pudding?" Ken sputtered. "I thought you said it was Brown Betty."

Now it was my turn to smile.

"Hmmm. I must have pulled out the wrong recipe. Still want seconds? You said you didn't do puddings in any way, shape or form." I stifled a giggle, as Ken's frown morphed into a grin.

"Now I can't say that anymore," my amiable husband replied as he handed me his dish.

Grandma always said the way to a man's heart was through his stomach. And I had been convinced Ken would love her old-fashioned dish if only I could coax him to taste it. Grandma also taught me that results are what count...it's not how you start but how you finish. I'd started with good intentions, albeit a little loving trickery, and ended with a satisfied spouse.

There's more than one way to skin a cat, I've heard. Wait...did Miguel Cervantes say that? No...I think it was Grandma.

Terri Elders

GERTIE'S APPLE BREAD PUDDING

Terri Elders

Ingredients

4 cups soft bread cubes

¼ cup raisins

¼ cup chopped walnuts

2 cups peeled and sliced apples

1 cup brown sugar

1¾ cups milk

½ cup butter

1 teaspoon ground cinnamon

½ teaspoon ground nutmeg

½ teaspoon vanilla extract

Directions

Preheat oven to 350°.

1. In a large bowl, combine bread, raisins, walnuts and apples.

2. In a small saucepan over medium heat, combine brown sugar, milk, and cup butter. Cook and stir until butter is melted.

3. Pour over bread mixture in bowl.

4. In a small bowl, whisk together cinnamon, nutmeg, vanilla, and eggs.

5. Pour bread mixture into prepared dish, and pour egg mixture over bread.

6. Bake in the preheated oven for 40 to 50 minutes, or until center is set and apples are tender.

32

THE CHILI CHALLENGE

My mother made the best chili in the world. "Spanish Chili," she would be quick to remind me. I don't know why Mom called it Spanish Chili. Perhaps she had gotten the recipe from Rosie, a neighbor whose family was originally from Spain.

Newly married, I asked Mom for her recipe. My husband had no idea what a treat he was in for. I pictured him sitting at the dining room table declaring, "You ought to open your own eating place on Restaurant Row!" I would think about that.

I sat down next to Mom, pencil in hand, my notebook opened to a clean, white page.

"Well…," Mom began. "You need a pound or so of ground beef, onions, red kidney beans, canned tomatoes, canned tomato paste, bay leaf (my Italian mother used bay leaves in all her recipes that called for tomato sauce), salt and pepper. You can add potatoes and carrots if you wish. Your choice. You cook all the ingredients in a skillet until done."

"That's it?" I questioned.

"That's it."

"But how much ground beef? Onions? Kidney beans? Tomatoes?"

"You just know," Mom declared. "It depends on how much chili you're making. You go by *feel*."

"You go by *feel*," my mind repeated.

It was a cool Saturday night. I got the skillet out and lined the ingredients on the kitchen counter. I chopped, mixed, sautéed, and stirred until I thought the perfect meal was ready to be served. I chose my best serving dish from the china closet, poured the heavenly chili from Spain into it, and set it on the table that my parents had given us for a wedding present. I wished I had remembered to buy film for my instamatic camera. This grand event should be recorded for posterity.

I filled our blue-and-white ceramic bowls with the incredible treat. After a couple spoonsful, I realized this didn't taste like Mom's. Not bad. But not Mom's. What was missing? What didn't I do right? It's got to be the kind of onion…or beans…or ground beef. I called Mom the next day.

"Oh, I use whatever's on sale. Or whatever I feel like."

"Feel?"

On my next trip to the supermarket, I attacked the produce section with a vengeance. White onions. Red onions. Brown-skinned onions. Which kind?

Next, the meat counter. Lean ground beef? Beef with some fat? What was on sale? Or maybe it was the kind of beans?

The following day I approached the Spanish chili challenge like I was competing for the grand prize in a national Chili Cook-off. The results were still not quite like Mom's — but better than before.

As the years went by, my husband and children enjoyed the chili I made from Spain. They never complained. And sometimes, they asked for seconds. But I knew it didn't taste like the chili that came from my mother's kitchen.

And then one day – Bingo! I nailed it! Just like Mom's.

"Okay," I said to myself. "What did I do? What did I buy? Maybe it was the potatoes, carrots, onions, beef." I couldn't remember exactly. But it didn't matter. So what if it wasn't exactly like the recipe I grew up with? I had all the delicious memories of sitting around the dinner table with my Mom and Dad, my sisters and brother. And now my husband, children and I were making memories of our own.

I say, "Compliments to the chef! Time to open Lola's Family Restaurant." I'll proudly hang a sign on my front door:

OPEN FOR BUSINESS!

COME RIGHT IN. TAKE A SEAT.

TODAY'S SPECIAL: MOM'S SPANISH CHILI.

ENJOY!

Lola Di Giulio De Maci

MOM'S SPANISH CHILI

Lola Di Giulio De Maci

Ingredients

Note: Amounts of ingredients may vary according to how much chili you want to make. Just "go by feel."

2 pounds ground beef

1 large onion

1 can (1 pound 12 ounces) tomatoes

1 can tomato paste (+ ¼ can water)

1 large can kidney beans, undrained

bay leaf

salt and pepper

potatoes and carrots (optional)

Directions

1. Brown beef in skillet with a little oil.

2. Before beef is thoroughly done, add onion and cook until transparent.

3. Add tomatoes, tomato paste and water, bay leaf, salt and pepper.

4. If adding carrots, do so at this time.

5. Cover and simmer about one hour.

6. If adding potatoes, dice and add one-half hour before done.

7. Add beans last ten minutes.

33

From Guacamole to Humble Pie in 30 Easy Minutes

The potluck. Where every home cook loves to strut. Best food forward. So when invited to a carry-in, I pondered a dish to flaunt. Brownies? *Too blah.* Meatballs? *I'm above beef marbles.* Salad? *Nobody eats carry-in salad except bunnies.*

No! This perfectionist needed a showstopper.

Two weeks I mulled.

Guacamole! *Perfect.*

I hit upon this the night before. No problem. Work 'til five, hit the grocery, then in a mere half-hour, chef my way to potluck prominence.

Next day, I strode into the store, bypassing the cheerful red grocery baskets. The produce section beckoned like a dear friend.

Jalapeno. Check.

Cilantro. Check.

Lemon, onion, garlic. Thanks, old friend.

Finally, the avocados.

I squeezed. And squeezed. The fruit, and my luck, didn't give an inch. Ever have a friend like that? Who's got your back?

With the clock ticking, my arms tiring, and my cilantro slipping, I selected three specimens that seemed least likely to break my toe.

I hustled home and began slicing one. *Cr-u-u-nch.*

Um, shouldn't avocados *squ-u-e-lch*?

I dug with a spoon…and produced a dent. In the spoon.

I whipped out a serrated knife. Cut through avocado skin only, not my own. Fortunately, before oiling my chainsaw, I remembered the microwave. Saved by the mush-maker, the melter of all foods fatty. *Beep, beep, beep.* Exuding hope, I opened the microwave — to steaming *cr-u-u-nch.*

Sweat beaded on my forehead.

Ten minutes left.

The food processor!

I lugged out the 80s-era behemoth, hacked ragged clumps from the peel and tossed them into the processor bowl. (Okay, okay, some peel went in, too.) But despite 700 watts, 300 hp and a can-do attitude, my reliable Cuisinart managed only avocado rice-lets.

Desperate, I plunged my hand past the industrial blades, squeezed the bits, prayed for *squ-u-e-lch* and produced a mound that — you guessed it — *cr-u-u-nched.*

I kicked the Cuisinart, shoved the avocado and my pride into the disposal, and grabbed a dusty jar of salsa (made in New York City). *Everyone likes chips and salsa,* I consoled myself as I floored the accelerator. *I won't be the princess of the potluck, but I'm still contributing.*

Upon my arrival, the host graciously accepted the humble product of my perfectionism and deposited it on the countertop beside a bowl of fresh, homemade salsa.

Sigh.

I had tried to strut, but instead put the best *fool* forward. Yes, I could teach a class on "Going from Guacamole to Humble Pie in 30 Easy Minutes." The point? Sometimes heartfelt participation matters more than an attempt at prideful perfection.

All it took for me to learn that lesson were some granite avocados!

Jaclyn S. Miller

NEARLY PERFECT GUACAMOLE

Jaclyn S. Miller

Ingredients

3 *ripe* avocados, mashed smooth (preferably Haas avocados)

2 tablespoons fresh lemon juice (or lime juice)

2 tablespoons cilantro, medium chopped

1 medium clove of garlic, minced

½ medium onion, chopped

1 medium tomato, diced

1 jalapeno, finely chopped

¼ teaspoon salt

dash fresh ground pepper

Directions

1. Stir all ingredients together well.

2. Let flavors blend, covered, for about an hour in fridge.

3. Taste and adjust salt (and perfectionist attitudes) if needed.

Serve with tortilla chips, celery stalks, and great humility.

34

DIRECTIONS MAKE
A DIFFERENCE

K en and I had been married for only a few months when he decided we needed to have his parents and brother over for dinner. I knew how to cook, but preparing a meal for several other people while under the pressure of impressing family terrified me like Frankenstein's Monster was staring me in the face.

After the invitation was extended, he informed me he told them all we were having a turkey.

Really?

A turkey? It's summer, not Thanksgiving. Why a turkey?

I didn't get an answer; just a twenty-pound frozen turkey brought home from the store. I looked at that turkey the size of three newborn babies and then at my apartment size oven. No way was it going to fit.

Not only that, but I didn't have a roasting pan that would hold the bird. I was wishing the Grinch would come and steal our roast beast and then I wouldn't have to face the dilemma of cooking it.

The dinner date was quickly approaching so I started reading the directions. This pan of poultry was huge and would take at least a week in the refrigerator to thaw.

I had purchased a disposable foil baking pan to accommodate the size of the turkey. I started the preparation by rinsing the poultry and running my hand into the cavity looking for the giblet package that I knew was in there. I found the neck bone and wondered why the rest wasn't there. "Hmm, maybe they don't put those in the birds anymore," my assuming mind thought.

I proceeded to season and baste the anticipated feast and after removing one of the oven racks I barely got the creature inside.

The bird's skin was almost touching the top of the oven and I hoped it wouldn't catch fire.

Several hours later it was time to get the summer Thanksgiving feast out of the oven. The hot pan was too heavy for me to handle alone so I had to call for reinforcements from the one who forced this punishment on me. However, after viewing Tom's perfectly browned skin I was proud of this offspring of mine for turning out so well.

The table was set with our best china and silver and the big bird was placed on my wedding gift platter. The knife was laid to the side awaiting the carving by my husband. My ears could already hear the accolades of what a good cook I was as I anticipated the family's first view of the magnificent poultry gracing the table.

We sat at our places and gave thanks. The usual dinner conversation was shared while Ken started the carving. The juicy bird smelled delicious. Slices of turkey were placed on plates and passed from one to another to complete the serving of everyone. Forks clinked against plates and casseroles complimented the meat.

The idyllic atmosphere was shattered when my brother-in-law looked at his plate and said, "What's that?"

We all peered toward his plate then checked our own. Ken looked back at the turkey he had been carving and saw an addition to the main dish. Small pieces of plastic were clinging to the meat.

I wanted to slink under the table as quickly as water down a drain, but I was stuck to my chair.

"Uh, I think you cooked the giblets with the turkey," my husband said while holding up a mutilated bag dripping with juice.

"No way, I checked and the neck is all there was."

After looking at the location of the now overdone plastic bag, I discovered the Butterball had two bags of innards in it and I had only looked for one. I didn't check both ends of the bird.

I knew no one would ever want to eat my cooking again and I wished time would speed up so this evening would be over. After we picked around the foreign object, we salvaged the rest of the bird and had plenty to eat. After all, there was twenty pounds of it.

It was a long time before I wanted to tackle another turkey again, but when I did every opening the bird had was checked before putting it in the oven. While I thought I had thoroughly read the directions, I found out my mind hadn't absorbed the content because I thought I already knew where the giblet package was. The thought didn't occur to me to look in other places.

I can do the same thing when reading the Word of God. Instead of skimming over certain verses because they are so familiar to me, I need to let my mind absorb the words as if I have never read them before. Following the directions God gives us prevents us from swallowing a foreign doctrine the way my family almost swallowed foreign objects with our dinner.

Whether it's giblets or decisions of life — directions make a difference.

Barbara Latta

35

SPICE OF LIFE

A gourmet cook, I have every herb and spice.
All of their names please me twice.
I savor the flavor of their double entendres
as much as I enjoy the complex aromas
that rise from the dishes I create.

While I cook, I meditate:

I'll take basil to town; he's salt of the earth.
Curry favor with the sage in the saffron robe,
but treat him gingerly; he carries a mace.

Open sesame!
Grandpoppy, allspiced up
and out in the chili air,
opens the gate of the sty;
the pig with cloven hoof
must be fed on thyme.
Rosemary (that pig) roots for
an American Indian arrow, or
maybe an East Indian turmeric paper
on taking a powder.

The leaves (all in mint condition),
cilantro, bay, dill, marjoram,
tarragon, parsley, oregano,
sway toward the loam-smell rows.
Down them Grandma casts seeds:
anise, cardamom, carroway,
celery, coriander, cumino,
mustard (you can believe in that);
everything a good cook needs.

Hovering trees offer berries:
junipers are great when sauced,
and — I do not hallucinate —
the nutmeg falls to ground
with cinnamon all around.
Be careful; don't bark your shin!
Vanilla beans dangle like spangles;
fine orange peel, like the rest,
yields olfactory zest.

Oh, I almost left out those who
contribute a gas to our lives;
the underground terrorists,
those ripe-smelling, good-taste enhancing
slippery guys: onions, garlic, and chives.

I shun inorganic chemicals,
but I use alum and cream of tartar.
Ooops! Tartar? Reminds me
of those bad Tatars in history,
but it does rise to the occasion
in baking and wine making!

Finally, for you I pepper this paeon
with color:
black, white, red, and pink;
and then with warmth:
paprika and cayenne.

I'm cookin' again!

Cybele Sieradski

Macaroni 'n Cheese

Cybele Sieradski

Makes 6-8 Servings

Ingredients

4 tablespoons butter

3 cups large elbow
macaroni

4 tablespoons flour

1 teaspoon salt

2 cups milk*

1 tablespoon olive oil

1½ 8-ounce bricks extra
sharp cheddar cheese

½ tablespoon coarsely
ground black pepper

1 8-ounce bag shredded extra
sharp cheese

1 great big pot of water

1 medium saucepan

1 3-quart casserole dish,
buttered

*About the milk: Usually, I have only 1% milk on hand (sometimes 2%). That's not good enough for Mac 'n Cheese. So I get wild, and use a mix of milk and half-and-half. I have used as little as only ¼ cup of half-and-half, and (with 1% milk) as much as a whole cup of half-and-half. Let your conscience (or your taste buds) be your guide!

Directions

Preheat oven to 400°

1. Before you cook the macaroni, prepare to cook the sauce. Measure the 2 cups of milk, and slice the 1½ bricks of cheese into slices about ⅛-inch thick. Have the flour and pepper handy, as well as the bag of shredded extra sharp cheese.

2. Fill the great big pot ¾ full of water and add the salt and

olive oil. Bring the water to a full, roiling boil. Add the macaroni and stir it to be sure none of it sticks together. Return it to a full boil, then reduce the heat just so it doesn't boil over.

3. Set a timer for 9 minutes. When the timer dings, capture an elbow and eat it, to be sure that it is just barely cooked (al dente), and not yet mushy. If it is "right," drain the macaroni and set it aside, preferably back in the empty great big pot with the lid on, where it can stay warm.

4. While the macaroni is cooking, in a medium saucepan, melt the 4 tablespoons butter. Into the butter smoothly blend in the 4 tablespoons flour, then slowly add the 2 cups milk. This mixture will not be thick, like gravy. That's okay. Add the slices of cheese, 3 or 4 at a time, stirring all the while to melt the cheese slices. They will thicken the mixture nicely. When the cheese is all melted, add the black pepper.

5. If you put your macaroni back in the great big pot, you are in luck. Stir it around (it will have got a bit sticky), then pour the sauce over it and stir it some more to coat all the macaroni with cheese sauce.

6. Pour it all into the buttered casserole dish. Sprinkle the top with the shredded extra sharp cheese.

7. Put the casserole in the center of the preheated oven and bake until it is bubbly and/or the cheese is nicely browned. You are ready to serve and eat the Mac 'n Cheese!

Some things you can add to Mac 'n Cheese: diced tomatoes, sliced green or black olives, pimientos, minced hot peppers, sliced hot dogs, pepperoni bits, ham cubes, bacon bits, and much, much more!

36

GOD AND
THE NUMBER THREE

There's something about the number three that God loves. There's the Trinity — God, Jesus, and the Holy Ghost. Gideon went to God three times and put out the fleece to make sure God was talking to him. Jesus rose from the grave in three days. Peter denied Christ three times, and there are many more examples too numerous to mention.

I once heard Jill Briscoe, an evangelist speaker, share with her audience how she'd tried to launch a neighborhood Bible study when living in London. The Lord told her to go out and canvas the neighborhood while strolling her child and ask all of the women to come to her Bible study one night during the week.

She cooked and baked all day and when the night arrived, not one lady showed her face. Jill cried and trudged back to God. "Lord, I did what you told me to do and no one showed." The Lord replied, "Go back and ask again."

Trying to be obedient, Jill ventured out the second time and asked everyone again. This time, some were so embarrassed they'd told her they would come and didn't — hoping the other neighbors would go — that they said they would come the next time. There was one blind woman who stated she didn't get out after dark. Jill thought that odd but shuffled on to the next house. And to the next. And the next. One door opened to reveal a deaf woman and Jill shouted her invitation not knowing if she'd been heard.

She slogged back home and as the Bible-study day arrived, she baked and cooked all over again. Still no one showed. She cried, went back to God and he said, "Go out a third time." She slung some more tears. "God, I can't go a third time!" God was relentless and told her to go so she gathered her wounded pride, and fluffed up stalwart courage to troop out the third time.

That night, two women showed. The deaf woman was leading the blind woman. Great, Jill thought to herself. One can't read the scripture and the other can't hear it!

What mattered — she was obedient. Finally, she did make headway with the two women. They seemed to be *getting the gospel.* She shouted it from the rooftops to the one and tried to paint a clear visual picture to the other. Eventually, her home ministry blossomed into a gathering of eighty women.

When I heard Jill tell that story I reasoned that I would have loved to have had someone invite me into their home when I was a young mother, to be fed physically as well as spiritually, and not have to bring food or wash a dish.

After I'd volunteered at Precept Ministries to learn how to teach one of Kay Arthur's 40-minute Bible studies, I decided to do something similar to what Jill Briscoe did. Maybe they wouldn't mind my teaching them if I plied them with good food. Soup and salad.

That's what I'd prepare! Easy and quick using fine china and crystal. Make them feel like queens.

Then fear crept in. Not a valiant warrior, I wondered, "What if no one shows?" My family would be eating soup until the next week! I invited ten people and paced the kitchen floor close to the window, terrified no one would come.

Tears dripping, I schlepped back to God pleading, "Lord, I'm not Jill Briscoe. You have one shot at getting me to do this. Someone had better show the first time because I don't have the faith Jill Briscoe has to ask again."

I wasn't married to a preacher, either, and Jill Briscoe was. Like that really mattered to God. I figured she had more faith than I did. More than likely, most of the time, I was probably from the same gene pool as doubting Thomas.

As I watched the clock and fretted, finally, seven women wheeled into my driveway, driving chariots of fire and right on time. I wiped my eyes and washed up odd dishes at the kitchen sink, thankful for my angels of mercy.

I planned on a forty-minute study — getting the women out of there within the hour so those who were pressed for time could return to work.

One young woman was a teacher; the principal of her school allowed her to come to the study because he was also a Christian. Another mom was an attorney; she scheduled her court cases around the study. Another lady grew up in the denomination of her brothers but had converted to another Christian denomination when she married; employed by her brothers, to get time off during office hours, she told them she needed to attend a *meeting* rather than a Bible study, otherwise they wouldn't have excused her to attend a function that wasn't of their denomination.

What initially was to be a one-hour study turned into two hours for some. We hashed and rehashed scriptural truths and had a wonderful time doing so. One attendee dropped out but I never had less than five.

I prepared a different soup every week and arranged fresh flowers on the table to brighten everyone's lunch. When my front door opened, they were assailed with smells of comfort. Who could resist potato bread and cheesy potato soup? Salad and bread left over after supper could be taken to shut-ins.

I photocopied recipes of each lunch and left them on the table for those who wished to try the soup recipes for their families. Kay Arthur was gracious enough to send me her favorite soup recipe to prepare one week. I was delighted to be able to pass it on to *my* ladies.

Not only was the study uplifting for me and the others, my smiling daughter walked in one day and said, "You know Mom, I love coming home from school to fresh flowers every Wednesday, knowing the house is going to smell like some new yummy soup."

Her favorite recipe was my very own Get Lucky Soup. That's the one where I threw all of the refrigerator leftovers like chicken, potatoes, and carrots into a rich creamy milk laced with butter — sort of my gourmet signature soup.

When shopping for the ingredients for recipes and purchasing fresh flowers at the grocery, I lingered around exotic orchids before wistfully moving on to select roses and daisies. Every time I thought, *I would love to have an orchid but they are so expensive and I don't have the green thumb for indoor plants,* and I reluctantly passed them by.

Warm weather was teasing the air. One night I thumbed through a nursery catalog I'd received in the mail. Stopping at an interesting page I thought, "Mmmmm, lilac bush. I don't have a lilac bush in my garden. I need to purchase one." I kept my dream flowers to myself thinking maybe one day I might splurge and dig a hole for my heart's desire.

I went onto other Southern reading material where I read, "Watch out when it says 'lo and berhol' in the Bible 'cause the Lawd's getting ready to do something big."

Well, *lo and berhol,* on the last day of class, one lady showed up with a lilac bush for planting in my garden and two other women splashed in with an exquisite white orchid. Another brought a beautiful silver prayer necklace. No one knew that I'd been secretly wishing for the plants because I hadn't breathed it to a soul. The necklace was a bonus! I was stunned and speechless. Three gifts! I hadn't expected a thing except for making it to the end of that class with people still coming and me still standing!

After God had enlarged my territory as he did for Jabez in 1 Chronicles, he'd blessed me indeed and I was still amazed over those two particular gifts — gifts God knew I'd wanted though I'd never verbalized my wishes out loud. I'd never expected a thing in return for what I was doing. I only tried to bless others.

I discovered when I was obedient, God loved favoring me with a double portion — just as he did Job for all his trouble — and then delighting me with something he knew I would enjoy.

Now that my faith has grown, who knows — I might go for

three tries for the next Bible study if I'm rejected the first time and no one shows. Faith as strong as Jill Briscoe's and a relationship with God is something that is planted, watered and harvested. Like a seed, it just grows.

And *Lo and Berhol* — I think there is just something about God and the number three!

Vicki H. Moss

Potato Soup

Vicki H. Moss

Ingredients

1 tablespoon unsalted butter

1 cup chopped onion

2½ tablespoons all-purpose flour

3 cups chopped potato (about 1 pound)

1¼ cups heavy cream

1 cup sour cream

¾ cup fat-free, lower-sodium chicken broth

½ cup water

½ cup (2 ounces) shredded reduced-fat sharp cheddar cheese or cubed Velveeta or slices of American cheese cut up

⅛ teaspoon ground red pepper

2 tablespoons chopped green onions

3 tablespoons chopped fresh parsley

3 strips well-cooked bacon

Directions

1. Melt butter in a medium saucepan over medium-high heat.

2. Add onion to pan; sauté 5 minutes or until onion is tender.

3. Sprinkle with flour; cook 1 minute, stirring onion mixture continuously.

4. Add potato, milk, broth, and ½ cup water to pan; bring to a boil.

5. Cover and reduce heat.

6. Simmer 10 minutes.

7. Add ½ cup reduced-fat sharp cheddar cheese (or substitute) and ground red pepper, or black pepper if you prefer.

8. Cook 2 minutes or until cheese melts, stirring frequently.

9. Top each serving evenly with 1½ teaspoons chopped green onions, parsley, and bacon.

37
April Fool's Day Prank

I have some great memories of April Fool's Day!

I couldn't wait to put salt in the sugar bowl. I would wait innocently at the breakfast table for my dad to put his customary two teaspoons of sugar in his tea mug.

As he drank the first sip and sputtered, "What's wrong with this tea?" I would laugh so hard... well, you know what happened! Every year I did this same prank and I thought he might become suspicious, but if he did, he played right along with my mischievousness. He continued to love me despite my crazy deeds. I was lucky that I had a dad who loved me unconditionally.

Dad was a great example of what our heavenly Father is like. Many people have a hard time understanding the unconditional love of God when their own dad wasn't so great. God's plan is that all dads would reflect his character. God wants the very best for all of his children. It's a love we may never fully understand, but all we need to do to receive it is ask.

"The LORD is like a father to his children, tender and compassionate to those who fear him" (Psalm 103:13 NLT).

April Fool's Day began in the 1700's in England with people playing jokes on one another. It is known by several different names in Europe, but it spread through Britain in the 18th century and caught on with many funny outcomes.

There are nothing but delicious outcomes and lovely memories when spending a special afternoon with friends. On a recent trip to visit my granddaughter, Nicole, we spent an afternoon in the kitchen baking fantastic Lavender Lemon Cupcakes. I think you will enjoy them as much as we did. Brew a pot of lavender tea to go with them.

Penelope Carleveto

LAVENDER LEMON CUPCAKES

Penelope Carleveto

Cupcake Ingredients

4 teaspoons lemon zest

¼ cup lemon juice

2½ cups cake flour

1½ cups all-purpose flour

4 teaspoons baking powder

1 teaspoon salt

½ teaspoon baking soda

1 cup buttermilk*

1 cup unsalted butter at room temperature

2¼ cups sugar

3 large eggs

½ cup sour cream or plain yogurt

Directions

Preheat oven to 350º

1. Line 24 muffin pans with cupcake liners.

2. In a large bowl, stir with a whisk, the cake flour, all-purpose flour, baking powder, salt, and baking soda.

3. Mix the buttermilk and lemon juice in another large bowl and set aside to use later.

4. Mix the lemon zest, butter and sugar together with an electric mixer and beat at low speed until the mixture is creamy and smooth.

5. Add eggs to the creamed mixture, one at a time, mixing well after each egg.

6. Add the sour cream or yogurt until smooth.

7. Add the flour mixture in two parts, alternating with the buttermilk and lemon mixture. Mix at low speed after each addition until all the flour and buttermilk mixture is gone, and stir until batter is smooth.

8. Let the batter rest for 20 minutes and then stir gently before adding to cupcake liners.

9. Fill each cupcake liner ¾ full then bake until the top of

the cake is firm, about 18 to 20 minutes. It is a good idea to insert a toothpick into the middle of each cupcake to make sure it is thoroughly baked.

10. Place the muffin pan onto a cooling rack for about 5 minutes, then remove the cupcakes to a rack until completely cooled.

*Buttermilk substitute – Stir 2 tablespoons of lemon juice or white vinegar into 1 cup of milk. This can be used in place of buttermilk in all recipes.

LAVENDER FROSTING

Step 1

Ingredients

2 tablespoons culinary lavender

2 tablespoons half-and-half

Directions

1. Combine half-and-half and lavender flowers and bring to a simmer.

2. Turn off heat and allow to cool.

3. Strain lavender from the half-and-half and set aside.

Step 2

Ingredients

½ cup unsalted butter, room temperature

8 ounces softened cream cheese

3 cups or more powdered sugar

Lavender mixture from Step 1

Directions

1. Cream together butter and cream cheese until combined.

2. Add the lavender-infused half-and-half until well mixed, then add powdered sugar and cream until lightly fluffy, about 5 minutes.

3. If frosting is too thin, add more powdered sugar. If too thick, add milk until desired consistency is reached.

4. Place the frosting into a plastic bag with a piping tip and pipe cupcakes in a swirl pattern.

5. Sprinkle each frosted cupcake with a small amount of dried lavender leaves.

38

MAKING MEMORIES WITH MY SWEET-TEA

For our fortieth anniversary, my husband, Milt, wrote in my card, "Let's go for tea for-TEA times during the next year." What a sweetheart! He knows I love teatimes with him. But forty outings in a year? That didn't seem possible.

But hurrah for us! We did it. Not in a year, but in a little over two years. On a gorgeous fall day with pumpkin-orange and golden leaves blowing in the wind, we drove to The Secret Garden Tea Room in Sumner, Washington, for our grand finale for-TEA-eth outing. We enjoyed a lovely teatime and sipped Pink Orchid and Almond Enchantment teas and nibbled on delicious goodies. As we drove home, feeling cozy and content, the crisp sunny day turned chilly, and the first snowflakes of the season fluttered down.

After arriving home, we sat by the fire and nibbled leftover desserts. The day had been sweet in more ways than one.

We reminisced about our forty outings and discussed what we liked about tearooms. "The ambiance and food are important to me," I said.

"And I appreciate good service," Milt chimed in.

I smiled. "I prefer tearooms that offer warm hospitality, where you almost feel like you're welcomed into a home."

My husband nodded. "The price is important too."

With my frugal farm-girl upbringing, I agreed. "Even when I buy dainty delicacies, I like to get a good value for my money."

We discussed the people we met or shared tea with that made our outings special.

My husband smiled. "I like having a cup of tea with Lydia." He knows how to charm me. And, yes, most of our outings were tea for two.

"Remember the lady we met from Crimea?" I asked. My parents had lived in Crimea, so we had an instant bond with her. The lady wondered if we might even be distant relatives.

"We also took Joan to tea for her birthday," Milt recalled. Yes, sometimes we combined our outings with treating a relative or friend to tea, which made a lovely gift for them and us.

Of course, there were jaunts when we included grandkids. Five-year-old Clara joined us for a ferry ride to a special tearoom in Port Gamble, Washington. "Oh, this is so fancy," she said as she touched the lace curtains. She dressed up with a hat and beads from the tearoom's selection and pranced to our reserved table, which was covered with starched linens. "There will be lots of treats, won't there?" she asked. And after she ate her fruit, dipped in chocolate fondue, she left with a happy, chocolaty smile.

Whenever we took road trips, we planned ahead and stopped at tearooms along the way. En route to Montana, we enjoyed tea in Spokane with friends at Brambleberry Cottage. On a trip to Oregon, we stopped at several tearooms, including Tea's Me, where we were served in their large gift shop where Christmas items are sold year round. We also traveled to Tamara's Gifts and Tearoom in Walla Walla, Washington, to meet for the first time with two publishers of my tea column. Tearooms are a great place to make new friends.

We arrived at Anna's Tearoom in Coupeville, Washington, on the last day it was open. The proprietor chatted with us, and I raved about the delicious Chocolate Satin Pie. "Would you like the recipe?" she asked. I gladly wrote it down. It's easy to make and may become your favorite decadent dessert.

Each adventure taught me new things about serving tea and inspired me to show hospitali-Tea in our home. These special teatimes also made my taste buds dance. But most of all, they created lovely moments with my Sweet-Tea.

Although we reached our milestone of forty tea outings some years ago, that hasn't stopped us from continuing these adventures. Now as our fif-TEA-eth anniversary approaches, we continue making warm memories over a cup of tea.

Lydia E. Harris

CHOCOLATE SATIN PIE

Lydia E. Harris

Smooth, rich, and delicious; just right to satisfy your chocolate craving.

Ingredients

1 ready-made chocolate piecrust

1 12-ounce can evaporated milk

2 egg yolks, beaten

2 cups semisweet chocolate chips (12 ounces)

1 teaspoon vanilla

Directions

1. Combine milk, eggs, and chocolate chips in pan over medium heat and stir constantly, until mixture thickens (about 5 minutes).

2. Stir in 1 teaspoon vanilla.

3. Pour the mixture into ready-made chocolate piecrust.

4. Chill.

5. When ready to serve, top with whipped cream.

6. If desired, garnish with nuts, shaved chocolate, or swirls of chocolate syrup. Or for the holidays, top with crushed candy canes.

Variations: Use milk chocolate chips for a milder, sweeter chocolate flavor. Add a layer of peanut butter on top of the piecrust before adding chocolate filling.

39

AUTHENTIC ENCHILADAS

I was born in Arizona where authentic Mexican restaurants could be easily found. My parents enjoyed take-out often, but told their three little daughters that we were too young to eat spicy food. We enjoyed TV dinners instead, while salivating at the delicious aromas of tacos and enchiladas.

When we became old enough to try Mexican food, of course we loved it! By then we lived in northeast Iowa and my parents had found an authentic family-owned Mexican restaurant. It was located in an old barn-style, dance hall building on the edge of town. It easily rivaled the local fast food taco place. The family restaurant operated on a budget too small for advertising, but word-of-mouth was effective. We ate there or ordered carry-out frequently, and it always seemed busy.

One evening we went to the restaurant and found it closed. A sign on the door announced it was out of business. We surmised the rent or maintenance stretched beyond the profit margin. We reluctantly drove to the Taco Place to get fast food that seemed much too Americanized for our tastes.

Many months later, we heard the family re-opened in a large, converted two-story home next to a funeral home downtown. They created seating on the main floor and in the finished basement. We gladly patronized their new location. Our favorite items on the menu, tacos and enchiladas, satisfied just as well next to a funeral home as they did in a barn setting.

Years later the family announced a final closing date. We didn't ask why they were closing, we just mourned the news. But my sister, with clear foresight, bravely asked for the enchilada recipe.

I still am surprised they gave it to her, but thankful. It's become the most-requested dinner item at my home. My children, who never set foot in the original restaurants, are happy to help make and devour them.

Janet Sobczyk

Authentic Enchiladas

Janet Sobczyk

Ingredients

3 tablespoons olive oil

3 tablespoons flour

2½ cups water

4 tablespoons chili powder

1½ teaspoons garlic salt

1 pound hamburger

diced onions, (optional)

10 small flour tortillas (may use the larger ones with more hamburger and cheese)

2 cups approx. grated cheddar cheese (or colby-jack or Mexican-blend), plus more to garnish

Directions

Filling

Preheat oven to 350°.

1. For the sauce, warm oil in saucepan.

2. Add the flour and brown briefly in oil, stirring.

3. Mix together the water and 2 spices. Add to the flour mixture and stir.

4. Bring to a boil and simmer for 10 minutes, stirring occasionally.

5. Meanwhile, brown the hamburger and onions in a skillet.

6. Drain off fat.

To assemble

1. Place enough sauce in a 9"x13" pan to thinly cover the bottom.

2. Lay tortillas out on a counter or table and evenly distribute hamburger and cheese on them.

3. Roll up tightly and place close together in the pan.

4. Pour remaining sauce evenly over the tortillas to coat well.

5. Bake 20 minutes at 350°.

6. Sprinkle tortillas with more cheese and let it melt before serving.

Serve with salsa, sour cream, and sliced black olives as garnish choices.

Side dish ideas: refried beans served warm with salsa and cheese, Spanish rice, and a black bean salad, or fresh fruit.

40

Bubblegum Pie

Thanksgiving has always been one of my favorite holidays. Every year, my extended family gathers at Grandma's house. It's a small place but we make it work with multiple tables and chairs sitting snugly against each other, leaving very little elbowroom.

There are three couples, plus Grandma, six grandchildren, and four great-grandkids. Usually, two or three of Grandma's friends join us as well. Because it's such a large crowd we have a potluck with families signing up ahead of time to bring turkeys, stuffing, cranberries, mashed potatoes, drinks, appetizers, and pies.

Typically, Grandma supplies the turkeys, Aunt Mina brings an appetizer, and Aunt Margaret brings the pies because she enjoys baking and is good at it. Everything else is split up among the rest of us.

Aunt Margaret usually makes four pies: Apple, Pumpkin, Mincemeat, and Sheer Bliss. The first three are standard fare, but Sheer Bliss is a real treat. It's a multi-layered pie that starts with a graham cracker crust. The first layer is a combination of chocolate chips, milk, and marshmallows melted together. It's quite dense. After that, there's a layer of bananas, then the pie is topped off with a layer of vanilla pudding mixed with whipped cream.

The first time Aunt Margaret made it for my Uncle Jim, she forgot to mix milk in with the chocolate chips and marshmallows. Every time you took a bite, you chewed, and chewed, and chewed because the marshmallows hadn't melted. So he re-named it Bubble Gum Pie, and the name has stuck.

Now it's one of the most popular pies at Thanksgiving and everyone makes sure they get a piece right away.

Milk makes all the difference.

Ellen Andersen

Sheer Bliss (Bubblegum Pie)

Ellen Andersen

Ingredients

1 cup vanilla wafer crumbs

½ cup chopped pecans

⅓ cup melted butter

2 cups miniature marshmallows

1 6-ounce package Nestles chocolate chips

¼ cup milk

1 small package instant vanilla pudding

1½ cups whole milk

½ pint whipping cream (not Cool Whip)

3 bananas, sliced

Directions

Step 1

Preheat oven to 375°.

1. Combine vanilla wafer crumbs, nuts, and melted butter.

2. Press into a 9" pie pan and bake at 375° for 5 minutes.

3. Cool.

Step 2

1. Combine marshmallows, chocolate chips, and about ¼ cup milk and melt. (The milk keeps it from getting too chewy.)

2. Pour into cooled piecrust.

3. Cool.

Step 3

1. Prepare vanilla pudding using 1½ cup milk.

2. Whip the whipping cream then mix with chilled pudding.

Step 4

1. After chocolate-marshmallow layer has cooled, slice bananas over the top.

2. Pour pudding mixture over chocolate and bananas.

3. Garnish with chocolate curls if you want to get fancy.

41

WHO WANTS TO COOK?

When our daughter graduated from high school, we decided to celebrate by heading to the beach. Dear friends, whose son had also graduated, joined us. We took them to our favorite condo in Garden City Beach, south of Myrtle Beach.

I recommend you assess certain facts before traveling with friends or family. We know everyone has idiosyncrasies; but we still need to be aware of them…and maybe it would be wise to have a good conversation with all parties because some things can be overlooked and some need to be addressed. There may be folks in the mix who are night owls and others who aren't. You need to set ground rules of how loud the television can be after 10 P.M., or who likes to cook and who doesn't — or who even knows how to cook for that matter. Enough said.

The six of us were actually a great fit and had a great time. We did experience a cooking issue, however. Not a bad one, but a scary one nonetheless.

I love to cook. When my family goes to the beach, we like to rent a condo so we can spend more time on the beach, then eat at the condo rather than stand in the long lines at the restaurants. The other lady in the group doesn't like to cook. Before we left for the trip, we all planned our week of who would cook each day and when. The other family wanted a day or two to experience all the seafood restaurants, and we planned for that. We were in agreement before leaving Ohio.

Everything went well until that one night.

The other lady was cooking hot dogs for the evening meal. She had been trying to talk the guys into tossing the idea and going out to a restaurant. I decided I wasn't getting into the discussion because I knew exactly what my hubby would say. I threw up my hands and laughed then said, "I'm going to take a shower and get this suntan lotion and sand off — you all decide what we're doing and I'll go along with whatever it is." And off I went to the shower.

All was well until I heard all kinds of yelling. "Fire!" Mumble, mumble. "Fire!"

In the shower, I wondered if they were playing. Were they serious? Who actually yelled fire? Should I be getting out? I listened a second or two and I didn't hear anything else, so I continued my shower.

"Fire! Seriously, come! Fire! Fire!" Mumble, mumble…stomp, stomp, running, stomp. Running, stomp.

Oh. Good. Grief! There must really be a fire. Great! I'm buck-naked and they are running out of the condo and nobody is telling me. What in the world?

I hurriedly try to get the shampoo out of my hair and turned off the water. I stepped out onto the towel and started putting my clothes on over my wet body.

Then I smelled it. Oh. My. Goodness! We *are* on fire and I can't get my clothes on over my wet body. Wait, somebody please tell me what's happening. Oh, somebody please help me.

Have you ever tried to put a bra on a soaking wet body…in a hurry?

I sort of got dressed, opened the door to the bathroom, and went out into the living room. I saw that the other five had gathered around the kitchen area and opened all the windows throughout the condo. It filled with the most sickening odor, no matter where you went in there. The smell burned your nose, and if you pinched your nose and breathed through your mouth, it burned your throat. I finally joined them in the kitchen and asked, "What is going on? I heard somebody yell fire?"

Nobody said anything.

I said, "Anybody?"

Finally, the lady cooking said, "Well, I lost my battle to go out for dinner and came in to turn on the stove to get the electric burners hot to boil the water for the hot dogs and mac and cheese. I didn't see that the stove had these thingies over the burners. I told you I don't cook, it's not my fault. I warned all of you."

I stood there stunned for a moment not knowing what to say. I finally looked at her and said, "Seriously, it's Wednesday…you haven't noticed those at all since we got here on Saturday?"

"No, I was trying to avoid this room. I thought if I didn't look at it, I wouldn't have to cook in it," she said, grinning ear to ear.

And her sweet hubby, who rarely says anything, mumbled under his breath — but loud enough to be heard — "Guess she figured if she burned up the stove we could go out for seafood."

At which point all six of us busted out laughing.

The moral of this story is simple. If you are going to travel with others, in the meal planning make sure the other cooks really do want to cook. Trust them when they say, "I'm gonna be on vacation and I don't want to cook." It will save you a fee from the rental company of $50 for burner covers that came from the dollar store that cost, well, a dollar. And the embarrassment of coming out of the bathroom with your clothes stuck pretty much where they landed when first put on.

Tammy Karasek

Beach Pasta Alfredo with Shrimp

Tammy Karasek

Ingredients

1 pound package of fettuccini (or your favorite pasta noodle)

4 tablespoons (½ stick) of butter

1 cup half-and-half (or skim milk)

½ cup freshly grated Parmesan cheese

salt to taste

a couple of grinds fresh black pepper

1 pound raw shrimp, peeled and deveined

4 tablespoons (½ stick) of butter

½ cup fresh minced parsley for garnish (optional)

Directions

1. Put water on to boil for pasta and cook according to package directions.

2. Once cooked, drain and place back in pot and cover to keep warm.

3. Melt 4 tablespoons of butter in small pan.

4. To melted butter, add milk and bring almost to a boil, watching for the bubbles coming to the surface.

5. While the milk and butter are warming, melt the other 4 tablespoons of butter in a medium sized skillet on medium high heat.

6. Once melted, add the shrimp and sauté about 3-4 minutes until they are pink/white with no signs of gray coloring. Be careful not to overcook though, or they will be chewy.

7. When the butter and milk mixture is almost to bubbling, pour over fettuccine and add the ½ cup grated Parmesan cheese, salt, and pepper, and toss gently until all pasta is coated.

8. Add the shrimp on top of the dressed fettuccine.

9. Sprinkle the minced parsley on top for color.

Serve with extra Parmesan cheese for those who prefer more.

We call this Beach Pasta Alfredo with Shrimp because every time we went on vacation to the beach, had this for dinner at the condo once during the week. We would buy fresh shrimp, and it was a very easy dish to put together. Also, by substituting half-and-half or skim milk for heavy cream, it's a little lower in fat.

42

WHERE'S THE GRAVY?

Southern gals know how to make gravy. It's one of those unspoken prerequisites for coming of age in the south and getting married to a Southern guy.

Types of gravy come in the boatsful — you've heard of the "gravy boat." Red-eye gravy (ham). Chocolate gravy. Turkey gravy. Tomato gravy. I'm referring to breakfast gravy, usually sausage-flavored, poured over piping-hot Southern biscuits.

For twenty years my husband, Mike, served as a youth pastor. He now holds the lead pastor position at our church. Mike grew up on Southern gravy, as did I. Many of our pastor friends often discuss whether there is food in heaven and if it's Southern favorites like pinto beans and cornbread…and gravy!

As a *good* Southern gal and pastor's wife, I learned how to make gravy early in our marriage. Over the years, I prepared Southern gravy countless times — Saturday morning family time and special occasions.

Still to this day, I often cook a Southern breakfast for dinner and I'm always serving gravy on holidays. Like some restaurants that serve breakfast all day and every day, Karen's Kitchen is always open for gravy.

Our Christmas morning family tradition is to have a huge Southern breakfast. My husband, my adult son and daughter, my son-in-law, and other relatives come to our home for this spread.

What I call "gravy trauma" occurred while making traditional gravy on one such occasion. Anyone who has made gravy can attest to the occasional splatter of grease popping out on a hand or arm. While I worked with a spatula for the right consistency, a large amount of hot, floured grease landed on the top of my left hand.

An immediate, intense burning sensation hit the nerve endings on my skin. Discolored in a disgusting brownish-green tint, it formed a big blister. Karen's Kitchen would not be serving gravy that day. Instead, a nasty burn served up a relentless dose of pain.

My husband worried I might never make gravy again, likening that to a real emergency situation. I'm happy to report I have made gravy since the "gravy trauma." But I knew I would not come out of the ordeal physically unscathed. I would have some semblance of a scar. No hiding the scar. No camouflaging. Clothing would not cover it. Cosmetics might help minimally.

The healing process took about six weeks. Today, I bear a scar on the top of my hand.

Healing from an injury — even after the completed process — often leaves a mark behind, a record that something happened there.

It reminds me of a friend who bears scars. Two scarred hands. Jesus bears scars on his hands, his feet, his side, and his back. Why? Because *something happened there.* Nails pounded into a wooden cross through his hands caused the scars there. A sword pierced his side. Flogging left stripes of scars on his back.

Christ suffered excruciating pain through beatings and crucifixion, dying on a cross so we could have eternal life.

He was wounded for our transgressions, he was bruised for our iniquities; the chastisement of our peace was upon him; and with his stripes we are healed. (Isaiah 53:5 KJV)

Karen Friday

Southern Gravy
Karen Friday

Ingredients

1 pound of pork sausage

all-purpose flour

1 can Pet Evaporated Milk mixed with

1½ cups water (You can substitute 2-3 cups of 2% milk for the can of evaporated milk and water)

Directions

1. Fry the sausage in patties until cooked through and seared on both sides.

2. Remove from skillet.

3. Keep 2 tablespoons of sausage grease/drippings in the pan. Save the reserve in case it's needed.

4. Put flour by heaping tablespoons into hot grease (med-high heat) 1 tablespoon at a time stirring constantly with a spatula to prevent burning. You want the consistency to be that of a roux, not too thick and "dry" and not too thin.

5. Add more flour or more grease as needed. There's no exact measurements with Southern gravy. It adds flavor to your gravy to let the flour mixture cook to a dark brown color, but don't let it burn.

6. Once the brown color is reached, pour in milk. Add milk in parts, stirring after each addition. Too much milk, and the gravy will not thicken. Not enough milk, and gravy is too thick. You can always add more milk as you go and a little water if needed.

7. Turn heat to simmer, and while gravy is simmering add salt and pepper to taste, and a pinch of sugar.

8. You can also crumble 1-2 pieces of your cooked sausage into the gravy.

9. Pour over piping hot Southern biscuits.

43

INTERNATIONAL MINISTRY
NO PASSPORT REQUIRED

However, as it is written: "What no eye has seen, what no ear has heard,
and what no human mind has conceived"—
the things God has prepared for those who love him—
1 Corinthians 2:9 NIV

As far back as I remember, I hated to cook. My mother, burned by hot coffee as an infant and wearing lifelong scars, did not allow children near the kitchen stove. By the time my sister and I reached an age Mom felt comfortable with our assistance, my interest was nonexistent and my sister's was limited. Therefore, Mom continued cooking, and the two of us cleaned. As a result, my poor husband lost weight when we first married. Eventually we mastered sufficient recipes for survival. Most proved edible.

However, once I tasted the opportunities in missions, my enthusiasm soared. Whether local outreach, chaperoning youth mission trips, or participating in international church partnerships, I knew I had found God's purpose for my life. I pictured myself devoting increasing amounts of time to these endeavors. All other activities revolved around mission trips, and we routinely set money aside for that purpose.

Yet, just when my schedule would allow expanded international work, life circumstances suddenly halted that plan completely. I'm unsure if or when such work can resume.

Less than a year before, a friend asked if we would consider keeping an international university student during Christmas break. My greatest concern — you guessed it — that's a lot of cooking. Other potential worries such as having a perfect stranger in our house, struggling with language barriers, or losing our privacy paled in comparison.

God definitely has a sense of humor and knows us so much better than we know ourselves. We loved those six weeks. Some of our best times revolved around grocery shopping, planning menus, and teaching her to cook. Wonders never cease!

She began inviting a few of her friends for meals, and the guest list kept expanding. Through trial and error we discovered several recipes they preferred. They enjoyed having a home away from home and participating in our daily routine, including kitchen cleanup — my old job. Perhaps they savored my culinary creations since their alternative was mass produced cafeteria meals and instant noodles.

Nevertheless our time together began to change my perspective. Increasingly I looked forward to cooking for these young people who had captured our hearts and become a part of our family.

Imagine my surprise at the first recipe request!

Our guest list changes as students leave and new ones enroll. Numbers vary from one to forty. We maintain contact with several no longer here. One returns for a visit every year.

Perhaps those international mission trips I saw as God's plan for my future were, in reality, preparation for our ultimate purpose. Whatever the future holds, I keep on cooking, loving, and praying for them all.

Increasingly I realize that God sees our world as one great community that hungers for eternal food. Christ compels us, as his followers, to feed our neighbors wherever they live and whatever the circumstances.

Diana C. Derringer

Recipe for International Ministry

Diana C. Derringer

Ingredients

1 cup of time

1 cup of flexibility

1 cup of friendship

2 cups of respect

1 heaping cup of fun

a dash of humor

assorted spices as desired

½ teaspoon of second language skills (optional)

2 cups of faith

2 cups of love

Directions

1. Combine time, flexibility, and friendship.

2. Blend well with respect.

3. Stir in fun and humor.

4. Flavor with spices to match guests' tastes and customs.

5. Add second language skills, if available.

6. (Additional humor may be required.)

7. Coat everything with faith and love.

This generously serves a growing family. Multiply as needed.

44

IS THIS THREE-QUARTERS?

Steal with your eyes." I remember my college English professor, Mr. Mansergh, telling me that when I complained about not being able to think of anything to write about. It's just another way to say, "Watch and learn," or "Be observant."

The more I thought about Mr. Mansergh's words the more I realized how much I had learned by watching my mother.

Mother was a wonderful cook. So many scrumptious delicacies originated in her kitchen. When I was a young child, she had me stand on a chair beside her and watch as she prepared the next meal or a batch of cookies. Sometimes she assigned me a task, suitable for my age — drop in the chocolate chips, keep the mixer bowl turning, grate the cheese, stir the ground beef in the skillet. I was well into my adult years before I realized there was another measurement for vanilla besides a "capful," because Mother always said, "Now add a capful of vanilla."

Wouldn't you know, when I had children, my daughter, Tina, came equipped with a totally different temperament than mine. She wanted no part of standing on a chair beside me while I chopped, stirred, fried and concocted. Her little mind and body ran full-speed ahead and did not light on anything long enough to observe and learn from me.

But Tina loved to do her kind of cooking. When she was a little older I let her take ingredients from the cupboard and cook. Whatever she made was undoubtedly heavy on the brown sugar. It was always quite soupy — never the same twice — beige in color, and swimming in chocolate chips, nuts and raisins. No one knew what it was, but she had been cooking, experimenting with the tools and ingredients found in my kitchen. I believe that the kitchen is a laboratory for learning math, reading and chemistry. I didn't want to discourage her.

As Tina moved through lower elementary school grades, she

developed her own basic reading and math skills. Eventually, she began to follow simple cooking directions: how to prepare macaroni and cheese out of a package, for example. She could be trusted with the stove, oven, and microwave when an adult was at home. She continued to raid my cupboards making her special unique blends.

When she was in fifth grade, I needed surgery. I was going to be home after one day in the hospital and could supervise the children, but would be confined to bed much of the time.

While I was resting, Tina came in and asked if she could surprise her dad and make him some chocolate chip cookies. "Yes," I said. "But I want you to follow the recipe on the package of chocolate chips. Will you do that?"

"Okay," she said.

"If you have any questions you can come ask me."

"I will," she assured me.

I must have dozed off because the next thing I knew there was a Pyrex measuring cup pressed against my nose. "Mom, Mom, is this three-quarters?"

I pushed her hand back far enough from my face to focus on the small finger pointing to the red line on the side of the cup. "Yes. That's three-quarters. Good job with your fractions," I said reinforcing her struggles for success in math class.

Tina bounced out of the room. Maybe it was my praise that made her extra joyful or perhaps she had been helping herself to the chocolate chips. Who knows? I felt a certain confidence in her recognizing when to ask for help and also her growing abilities in both math and life skills.

Soon the house began to fill with the wonderful aroma of chocolate chip cookies. I thought I might actually have to break my "No eating in bed" rule and have Tina bring me a couple cookies.

Soon, she came in and offered, "Mom, my cookies are done. Do you want one?"

"No, you made them for your dad. I'll let him have the first one. When he gets home, I'll get up for dinner and have one then."

I heard her meet her dad at the door with her cookies. She kept saying, "They're kinda hard, harder than the ones Mom makes."

"I'll eat one now and have more after dinner," her dad said. "This is a hard cookie. But it's good."

I could tell by the way his voice became hoarse and hesitant, something was wrong.

When I came to dinner Tina said, "Dad likes my cookies, but I don't know why they are so hard."

Well, I had been in bed thinking about this. "When you asked me about three-quarters, what did you put in them?"

"Baking soda," she replied sounding very sure of herself.

Quiet descended on the room for a few moments.

"I'll have another cookie now," her dad said. "Then I'm going to take the rest to work tomorrow and share with the guys in the shop."

"Good idea," I said.

I knew if Tina put three-quarters of a cup of baking soda in the chocolate chip cookie dough instead of three-quarters of a tablespoon as the recipe called for, the cookies were not only hard as a brick they tasted like something akin to laundry detergent, pickle brine, desert sand and belly-button lint.

I want to acknowledge right here and now that Tina did not have perfect parents, but that fiasco with the concrete chocolate chip cookies came close to being her dad's finest hour. The man had already choked down one of those cement cookies the minute he walked into the house. Then he consumed another, just to make his little girl happy. Plus, in order to keep me, his ailing wife, from having to eat one, he found a way to get the rest of them out of the house without letting Tina know they were headed to a dumpster.

No, not a perfect dad, but that day, I watched and learned something about parenting, as he stepped up to the cookie plate and became, not three-quarters, but a total super hero.

Mason K Brown

45

VENISON VICTUALS

Each year my husband, Kevin, and our two sons, Kyle and Hunter, prepare for their annual deer hunts — a ritual and also a rite of passage for young boys in the South whose ancestors depended on the fat of the land to survive before farming could provide crops to add to supper fare on America's early frontier. A couple hundred years ago, our region was filled with buffalo, wild turkey, panthers, mountain lions, wild boar, wolves, and deer herds that roamed through the woods and grasslands. Most of the wild animals are gone and turkeys were almost extinct not long ago. With fewer people hunting now, the turkeys have multiplied and can often be seen in the fields as we drive along our highways.

Since wolves are extinct in the South, there aren't many natural predators to cull the deer herds, so avid hunters are happy to help with this problem. Wild game in the freezer helps with the grocery bill and lean meat is also healthy for humans.

Not only is venison tasty and healthy, some fall with its deer season, the hunting provides bonding with families and friends. In early morning, the men in my family try not to wake me as they gather their gear and supplies so they can hit the deer stands before daylight when the four-legged critters start moving around to forage for food. When the day is done and meat comes home, it's time to cut and dress the venison for packaging.

But what about the gamey taste, some might ask?

If the deer is in "rut," the meat has a much stronger taste, but if not, then the meat can be soaked in milk for twenty minutes. Or water will also pull out the blood, making the meat taste better. Marinating the steaks or brining roasts in red wine, along with allspice and rosemary, also helps. The alcohol cooks out and the brine helps keep the meat moist. One thing you don't want to do is overcook venison. It also helps to bring the roast or steak to room temperature before cooking.

But what about killing Bambi, some might ask.

God made the animals for man's consumption; it provides a form of protein. Eating chickens, pigs, and cows that were raised in a stressful environment — cooped up pens for instance — can't be a good thing. A deer killed for human consumption — one that has matured and lived a good life up until it becomes meat on the table — goes through a much easier and less stressful death than one who has been chased by a pack of coyotes and torn apart while still alive.

What's the best part about deer season?

I get some quiet time all by myself. Or either a girl's day out! Whatever I choose to do for the day,

I always thank God for family traditions, my wonderful way of life in the South, and for providing daily food and sustenance for my family.

The rest of the story: If I'm cooking a roast or tenderloin in the crock pot I use McCormick's meat loaf packet. This addition was a culinary experiment I tried one day that made the meat taste great. Kevin fries tenderloin pieces (non-breaded) in a skillet with Dale's sauce. It's awesome! My main venison recipe is Deer Chili. It's a warm stick-to-your-ribs meal particularly great to eat after coming in from the cold.

Jessica H. Crowell

DEER CHILI

Jessica H. Crowell

Ingredients

2 pounds ground deer meat

2 large cans Bush's mild chili beans with sauce

1 packet Food Club chili seasoning

1 large onion

1 large green pepper

1 large can spaghetti sauce

Directions

1. Chop the onion and green pepper and brown in a skillet with olive oil until caramelized.

2. Place in a large cooking pot.

3. In the same skillet brown the deer meat.

4. Drain, and place in the pot with the onion and green pepper.

5. Add all other ingredients and cook until bubbly, adding water if needed.

Another option

After the onion, pepper, and meat are ready, place them in a crockpot and cook on high for 1-2 hours or so. It's faster on the stove but better in the crockpot! My family loves it. Garnish it with cheese and sour cream if desired.

46

A PAIR OF MERRY MOLLUSKS

A man taking basil from a woman will love her always.

Sir Thomas Moore

February 14 fell on a Tuesday in 1956, not a good-news day for us. Bob and I had hoped to spend our first Valentine's Day evening as a married couple at the Villa Nova, our favorite Italian restaurant. But I wouldn't get a paycheck until Friday, and we'd already spent Bob's GI Bill allowance on the rent and utilities for our tiny apartment.

"Don't worry, honey," Bob said that noon as we munched on our bologna sandwiches and apples on the shady patio of the cafeteria at Long Beach State College. "We'll celebrate tonight somehow."

An eternal optimist, Bob kept up the chatter as he drove me to the valve-manufacturing firm atop Signal Hill. I'd been lucky in landing a part-time job there, editing the company newspaper, a glossy monthly.

"I'll pick you up at 5. We'll have a cozy supper at home tonight. I think I'll have enough left after I fill up this old Pontiac's tank to buy a bottle of Chianti, and you can cook me up a Valentine's surprise."

It would be a surprise all right, I thought, trying to recall what remained in the pantry that I could make a meal of. Nonetheless, I forced a smile. At least we had each other, and we wouldn't be paupers forever. Bob intended to take the local police department exam in a couple of months, with the goal of joining the force by summer. We were certain he'd be assigned a swing shift, which would enable him to continue his police science studies at the college. He still had another year to complete for his degree.

At the office I conferred with Alisa, who worked in accounting.

"What can I make for a special supper tonight when I don't even have any meat?"

"Have you got any canned clams?"

"I think so, but that's hardly festive. Besides Bob doesn't like chowder."

Alisa grinned. "I'm talking pasta, baby. Pasta means amore… trust me, I'm Italian. Men love pasta. I'll give you my mom's recipe. And remember: If you don't have one thing on hand, just substitute another. Santo Valentino would approve!"

"Saint Valentine's Italian?" I cocked my head and furrowed my forehead. Somehow I'd vaguely thought of him as English, but realized I might have been thinking of a photo I'd seen of the statue of Eros in Trafalgar Square.

"Of course he's Italian! He's buried just north of Rome, near where my mom grew up."

Alisa scribbled down her recipe and I tucked the folded paper into my pocket.

That evening Bob dropped me off at our place.

"OK, honey. You see what you can conjure up, and I'll go get gas and some wine."

I opened the recipe as I checked its ingredients against the few cans and jars remaining on the kitchen shelf.

Canned tomatoes, canned clams, olive oil, parsley, oregano and my favorite basil. Si certo, I had them all. Plus a package of linguini. I always kept onions and garlic on hand, and still had half a loaf of sour dough in the breadbox. I even had a shaker of grated Parmesan. We'd have a feast. I rummaged around and found a red and white checked tablecloth and a couple of candles to make our kitchen table even more festive.

We ate every bite, and Alisa was right. It indeed was the food of love. Bob sopped up the last of the sauce with the last of the bread and sighed.

"My compliments to the chef. But I can't keep eating all this pasta if I want to get in shape for the police exam," he said, with a rueful shake of his head. He'd been running on the beach several evenings a week to prepare for the upcoming physical. "But tonight's special, so I think Saint Valentine will work his magic and make these calories not count."

"Did you know he's Italian?" I always liked to share my new knowledge with my amiable husband.

He looked at me as if I were demented. "What else would he be? What did you think?"

"Never mind." I sipped the last of my wine and smiled. "I'm just happy as a clam that you liked our dinner."

"And why are clams so happy?"

I was relieved he'd asked. I always enjoyed sharing such tidbits.

"People forget the second half of that saying. It's really 'happy as a clam at high tide.' I guess at high tide they are out there swimming around and not floundering on the sand where people dig them up."

"You're so smart," Bob said, laughing. "Wait right here while I get your Valentine's present."

He went into the bedroom and I heard him open a drawer. He came back with a homemade Valentine...a heart cut from the Sunday funnies, and a Hershey bar with almonds.

"Next year I promise a two-pound box of See's and a real Valentine," he said, giving me a hug.

"What do you mean? This is a real Valentine!" I opened it and read the verse he'd scribbled in crayon. Bob never had been noted for his poetic skill.

I read it aloud: "I will be your Valentine, if you will be my Clementine."

I gave my husband a puzzled glance. "Clementine? Didn't she drown?"

"Clementine's the name for those little mandarin oranges we saw at the Piggly Wiggly last Christmas. Remember how juicy and sweet and squeezable they were?" He squashed my hand to make sure I got the picture.

"And it's the only rhyme I could come up with at the moment for Valentine."

"I can think of another," I said, grinning.

"What's that?"

I giggled. "Frankenstein."

Bob hooted. "How about concubine? Or Palestine?"

We cleared away the supper dishes, merry as a pair of mollusks… at high tide.

Terri Elders

ALISA'S MOM'S PASTA AMORE

Terri Elders

Ingredients

1 pound package linguini

1 tablespoon olive oil

½ cup chopped onion

1 tablespoon minced garlic

½ teaspoon crushed red pepper

1 14.5-ounce can tomatoes

2 tablespoons tomato paste

2 6.5-ounce cans minced clams, undrained

1 tablespoon dried parsley

1 tablespoon dried oregano

1 tablespoon dried basil

salt, pepper to taste

Parmesan cheese, grated

Directions

1. Cook pasta according to package directions. Drain.

2. Heat olive oil in a large pot.

3. Add onion, garlic, and crushed red pepper and sauté 3 minutes or until onion is browned.

4. Stir in tomatoes and tomato paste.

5. Cook until thick, stirring constantly.

6. Add clams, parsley, oregano and basil.

7. Stir until heated through.

8. Serve atop drained pasta.

9. Sprinkle with Parmesan cheese.

47

THE ONE-LEGGED TURKEY

"Why don't we buy a turkey, and I'll cook it?" my husband Alan said. "We can eat some now and freeze the rest."

"Okay," I responded, knowing I would have to be involved.

Turkey day arrived. He took the huge bird out of the refrigerator and found the roasting pan. I put the box with cooking bags on the counter, added the flour container, and stepped aside to watch. This was his project.

He took the cooking bag directions and began reading. "First, cut off the drumstick."

"What?" I asked trying not to laugh.

"It says to cut off the drumstick."

My contorted face gave him a clue that something was wrong, so he admitted, "Maybe I read the directions wrong."

I picked up the booklet. "You looked at carving instead of cooking." I pictured him struggling to sever a stubborn, raw turkey leg and couldn't contain my laughter.

After listening to my cackle, he joined in.

He yanked the bag of partially frozen innards out of the turkey's cavity and laid them aside. I floured the plastic bag, and we wrestled the slippery bird into it. Alan cut slits in the top of the cooking bag and tied it shut.

Again, he picked up the cooking bag directions while I watched and waited. With a frown he read silently and then aloud. "In cold weather, it takes eleven hours."

I doubled over with tears streaming down my face. Finally, I grabbed the strange directions from his hand. With difficulty, I finally said, "This says cold water, not cold weather." Laughing, I continued. "You read the directions for defrosting."

He joined in with humor. "I wondered why the other column said four or five days."

I leaned against the refrigerator to keep from falling over as our chuckles continued. The soundless turkey rested on the counter. Between snickers, Alan was on a roll. "I wondered why cooking times would be different in cold weather."

After order was restored, we advanced to the technical part of the process. Like a lost little boy, he grew serious again. "What do we do now?"

I handed him the meat probe and stove instruction booklet. He began reading the oven directions, and after several steps and pushing many buttons, he figured it out.

With the turkey safely tucked into the oven, Alan resumed watching his football game, and I returned to the patio to read.

A couple of hours later, a wonderful aroma greeted me when I stepped back into the house. However, a sheepish Alan met me at the door and said, "I turned on the light to look at the turkey and hit the wrong button." He grimaced. "I think I might have turned off the oven."

I didn't doubt that at all which resulted in more laugher. Of course he didn't remember how to turn it back on. I repeated the instructions, he pressed the buttons, and the baking continued. I also pointed out the clearly marked oven light button.

When the timer finally buzzed, a beautifully browned turkey emerged from the oven. Each time we ate from that delicious turkey, we remembered the fun we had baking it.

Years later, when I recall that fun-filled day, I still envision what might have been — a blackened, shriveled, one-legged bird after it baked for eleven hours…in cold weather!

A dose of laugher can soothe difficult situations, warm the heart, and create wonderful memories.

Rebecca Carpenter

48

GRANNY'S BALONEY SALAD SANDWICHES

Granny took her well-faded apron off the hook on the pantry door, slipped it over her gray bun and tied the ribbon in the back. Then she took another apron, dropped it over my head and tied it for me. I stretched down to stick my hands into its pockets.

"Kurn Lynn," she said in her mountain twang, "if you'll run outside and rustle me up a few eggs, I'll dance at your wedding. Make sure it's the nests with only one egg."

"Why's that, Granny?" I furrowed my young brow.

"That's so you know they's fresh ones. If the nest is full, it means she's sitting on 'em and they have chicks inside. Now, hurry it up and get your coat on first. It's colder'n blue blazes out there."

I pulled my coat on and headed toward the door, thinking about how awful I'd feel if I cracked open an egg and found a half-grown baby chick inside. "Check under the hedge bushes. They like nesting up under there."

I slammed the door behind me and ran into the yard that backed up to the mountain. Chickens clucked and skittered away as I neared the hedge. A little rummaging around and I found the prize, a nest with only one egg. I kept searching until I found two more. She said a few eggs, but I wanted to make sure we had enough and found a fourth one over by the winter-bare pink rose bush. A thorn brought a spot of blood to my finger. I wiped it on my coat, grabbed the egg, and gently put it in one of the apron pockets with the others.

When I got back inside, Granny had a pot of water coming to boil on the coal-fired kitchen stove. I gently dropped the eggs into the water so it wouldn't splash, removed my coat, and washed my hands. The water nearly froze my fingers.

Granny stood at the kitchen table humming a church song as she stripped the red paper off a full-sized log of bologna. We called it baloney. She cut it into thick slices and let me cut those into chunks. I loved helping Granny cook. Living next door gave me lots of opportunities to help her around the house.

She took a smaller knife and made slices almost to the bottom of a sweet pickle. After turning it and cutting it the other way until it looked like a miniature green checker board, she sliced across it until there was a heap of perfect green pickle boxes. I hoped I could cook like Granny someday.

By the time we finished with our cutting up, the eggs had boiled long enough. Granny poured off the steamy hot water and ran some cold water over the eggs to cool them off a bit. She gathered them up, one by one, in her apron skirt and smacked them with the bowl of a spoon to crack the shells. I got to peel the shells off. They were still hot, but I managed. I sighed with relief when no boiled baby chicks were inside.

"Kurn Lynn, my purty little hen, are you ready to make baloney salad?" She always called me her purty little hen. It made me feel special.

"I shore am, Granny. Can I crank it this time?"

"We'll see if you've got the muscles for it. First, we have to get the ingredients into the grinder. If you'll get the mayonnaise out of the fridge I'll dance at your wedding. Be careful not to drop it."

I didn't know why she thought I would do things for her just so she would dance at my wedding. Besides, she'd already promised a hundred times or more.

"Okay, Granny." I didn't want to drop the jar and break it all over the floor. It was big and heavy, so I had to be slow and careful.

I love baloney salad. We only had it for Christmas Eve at

Granny's house. The party, with all the relatives who could travel back home to attend, would start in just a few hours. Thoughts of food, gifts, and Santa chased around in my head. Christmas was stressful on my young heart.

I climbed up in a chair on my knees so I could reach the grinder that was clamped onto the bare wood of the kitchen table. Granny guided me as I plopped cubes of baloney into the top and she cranked the handle only after my fingers were a safe distance away. I loved watching it come out the other end like baloney spaghetti and pile up in the pale green bowl underneath.

She sliced an egg down the middle and pushed it into the grinder and then some more baloney. I got to crank it. It was hard work. I had to push the handle with all my might and then pull it back toward me. My arm muscles hurt so much, I was glad when the last tidbits squeezed through the holes. Granny let me dip spoonsful of mayonnaise into the bowl next. Then we added the pickles and she stirred it all up.

I wanted to dig right into it, but I had to wait until later that night. We needed to make the sandwiches and stick them in the fridge first. Together we grabbed slices of Bunny Bread out of the yellow wrapper and slathered baloney salad on them. After topping each with another slice of bread, we cut them catty-cornered and arranged them on a turkey-sized platter.

When we finished the last sandwich, there was just a tad of the salad left in the bowl. Granny scooped it up and put it on the heel of the bread, folded it over, and handed it to me.

"Looks like you lucked out, Kurn Lynn. There's just a bite left over."

I smiled up at her as I grabbed it and bit off a hunk. Heaven.

Granny covered the platter with some tin foil and carried it to the fridge. Then came the clean-up. That part didn't excite me as much as the cooking. But, we got the table cleared off and wiped clean with a dishrag. Granny dismantled the meat grinder and took it to the sink to clean.

I wandered around the house to see the decorations. Mama had taped the Christmas cards all around the archway into the living room. Granny couldn't climb the ladder herself anymore. Christmas tablecloths covered the dining room table and buffet. In the living room, the newfangled silver Christmas tree sat at the front window. The lamp that came with it sat on the floor, angled up at the tree. When you turned it on, a round piece of glass shaped like a wheel with different colored pieces of glass in each of the spokes turned around and around. I wanted to turn it on so I could see all the pretty lights reflecting on the silver limbs, but didn't dare. Presents lay under the tree, waiting to be opened at the party. One of them had my name on it. I already knew what it was — underwear. Granny always gave me underwear. I wished it was something less embarrassing to open in front of all my relatives.

A yawn stretched my lips wide as I walked back to the kitchen. I'd had a busy morning. "Granny, do you need me anymore?"

"Not unless you want to lick the beaters after I mix up this fruit cake."

"Oh. Well… maybe I could stay a bit longer."

Karen Lynn Nolan

BALONEY SALAD SANDWICHS

Karen Lynn Nolan

Ingredients

1 big log of baloney

boiled eggs, cut in half
(About 4, according to
size of batch)

sweet gherkins, diced tiny

mayonnaise (Granny used
Miracle Whip)

white bread

Directions

1. Remove the red wrapper from the baloney log. Slice the baloney into chunks small enough to fit into the meat grinder. Grind into a large bowl.

2. Add halved boiled eggs to the grinder. Slicing the eggs in two first keeps them from exploding when you add them to the grinder.

3. Dice sweet pickles (as many as needed for the size of baloney log) and add to bowl.

4. Add mayo (Miracle Whip) until the right consistency.

5. Spread onto soft white bread, cover with another slice of bread, and cut catty-cornered.

6. Cover and place in fridge until cold.

49

The Great Soup Escapade

I recently discovered a secret ingredient even more important than cheese.

I know, I didn't think this was possible either. But it's true. And this secret ingredient is so unique, it is added not by the chef during cooking, but by the consumer right before eating. Here is the story of how I discovered it.

During Lent, my church hosts Lenten soup and sandwich suppers on Wednesday evenings before service. Each week, volunteers bring soup and the fellowship committee provides sandwiches. A dear friend advised that I should leave this particular volunteer effort to others, but I did not heed her warnings. I signed up to bring soup. Twice.

After my first effort tasted like soggy vegetables in water, I was determined to improve. I developed a plan.

"Please tell me your plan involves following a recipe," my friend said.

"Of course not, but I have an idea," I said.

"Why?" she cried. "Why do you do this to these nice people?"

"It's going to be good," I promised.

That morning I swung by the church on my way to work. I poured rice in my crockpot along with cooked and seasoned chicken, vegetables, diced tomatoes, and chicken broth. It smelled amazing. For once, I was going to make something good.

I fired up the crockpot and drove to work. All day long I daydreamed of simmering soup. Even from my office across town I could almost smell it. Chicken. Tomatoes. Herbs.

That evening I bounced into the fellowship hall, beaming at everyone in anticipation of the big soup unveiling. I was just in time. My crockpot was being carried out of the kitchen.

The sight stopped me dead in my tracks.

There, in her hands, was an erupting mound of primordial goo. It was expanding even as I watched, bubbling and clawing as though trying to escape from the pot.

"I wasn't…sure what to do— " she began, pot held at arms length.

I stared in horror at my masterpiece. The contents belched and spluttered. The mound was pulsing against the cover, inches above the pot.

"I must have put in too much rice," I said. And worse — the rice had cooked down to the consistency of paste.

"It will be okay," she replied, though the frantic pitch of her voice gave her away. She set the pot down quickly and grabbed a spoon, trying unsuccessfully to stir it.

People began lining up.

"What kind of soup do we have tonight?" Pastor asked.

"Well…I was going to call it Italian Chicken, but it's really more like a casserole," I said.

"Let's pray," Pastor said.

So we prayed, and then I bravely dug into my crockpot. If I was going to make these people eat my soup, then I was going to eat it, too. I pried a spoonful from the pot with an audible "thwuck."

And this, my friends, is where the secret ingredient gets added.

The first bite almost made me gag, and I've had years of practice with my cooking. But those people ate my soup without wincing and even made nice comments.

"We appreciate you bringing the soup tonight," they said.

"Your soup has a nice flavor," they said.

"My father always said soup was good if you could stand your spoon up in it," they said.

And I sat there thinking: Only the power of God could equip someone to say nice things about this soup.

I could learn a thing or two from these people. About humility. About gratefulness. About kindness.

"Be kinder than you have to be," I read once. "Because you never know what the other person is facing." I saw this demonstrated first-hand that night. They didn't have to eat my soup. They could have eaten sandwiches. They could have ordered take-out on their way home. But they did not. They added a secret ingredient that made even my soup palatable.

Kindness.

"Be kind to one another," Paul admonished (Ephesians 4:32 ESV).

We all have opportunities a dozen times a day where we could choose to be kind. It's far easier to be busy, harsh, self-centered, negative, stressed. But whatever we're facing right now, we are called to make a conscious effort toward kindness.

Take time today to be kind. And when your initial reaction is something other than kindness, please pause and remember that your situation could be worse.

You could be sitting down to a bowl of my soup.

Janet Beagle

Non-Recipe for Italian Chicken Soup Casserole

Janet Beagle

Ingredients

chicken, baked and
deboned

olive oil

herbs

Italian dressing (optional)

chicken broth

orange juice (optional)

1 bag frozen vegetables

rice

basil

oregano

parsley

red pepper flakes (optional)

ginger (optional)

cumin (optional)

cheese (optional)

Directions

1. Cook boneless chicken, and cut into bite-sized pieces.
   I recommend baking in olive oil and herbs or Italian
   dressing. Heat to an internal temperature of 165°
   Fahrenheit or until the smoke detector goes off. Whichever
   you prefer.

2. Pour chicken broth, a bag of frozen vegetables, and a can
   or two of diced tomatoes into a crockpot. Add the cooked
   chicken. If you're adventurous or short on broth, add some
   orange juice.

3. Add white or brown rice to taste. Use less for soup, more
   for casserole.

4. Sprinkle herbs for flavor and color. You can't go wrong
   with basil, oregano, and parsley. For a little extra kick, add
   some red pepper flakes. For an eastern flair, consider ginger
   and cumin. For true excitement, add them all.

5. Turn the crockpot on and simmer a couple hours until the
   rice is cooked. Or, cook all day to reduce your meal to a
   beautiful grey paste.

6. Ladle into bowls and serve with a side of fresh bread. Or, cut into squares and serve with plenty of drinking water. If all else fails, cover liberally with cheese.

7. Add kindness. And enjoy!

50

My Recent Social Life

I invited a man o'er to dinner.

The meal was no winner.

He eats no meat that is red,

so the appetizer went dead.

I served some cheese

that really did not please.

I put too much cayenne in the stuffing

for the mushrooms; we were huffing.

The broccoli was overcooked,

even that could not be overlooked.

The baguette had seen a better day;

we had to throw it away.

Dessert was not key lime pie —

the juice was forgot by little ole I.

In my state of rattled nerve,

the coffee I forgot to serve

The wine he did bring

was the only good thing.

Cybele Sieradski

ORDINARY SALAD DRESSING

Cybele Sieradski

Makes 1+ cup

Ingredients

¼ cup wine vinegar

1 large clove garlic, crushed or minced

¼ teaspoon salt

¼ teaspoon black pepper

½ teaspoon marjoram

1 teaspoon basil

1½ teaspoons parsley

¼ cup light olive oil

½ cup light oil (I use canola)

1 teaspoon Dijon mustard or dry mustard, (optional)

Directions

1. Put garlic in vinegar. Shake well.

2. Crush or grind herbs in mortar, with pestle.

3. Add herbs to vinegar. Shake well.

4. Add oils.

5. Shake well, again.

You can add crumbled feta or blue cheese to this dressing. As much as you like!

POP'S PECAN PIE

Cybele Sieradski

Ingredients

3 eggs, beaten

3 tablespoons melted butter

1 teaspoon vanilla

1 cup red-label (lite) Karo syrup

¼ teaspoon salt

½ cup sugar

1 cup broken pecans

1 deep-dish piecrust (frozen)

Directions

Pre-heat the oven to 350°

1. Remove the piecrust from the freezer to thaw.

2. Assemble the first six ingredients in the order given, mixing well.

3. Stir in the pecans.

4. Place thawed piecrust in pie pan.

5. Pour the mixture into the piecrust.

6. Put the pie on a cookie sheet (with a rim), and put it in the middle of the oven.

7. Bake for a minimum of 45-50 minutes.

It is (probably) done when the crust cracks. Check the center with a table-knife blade; it should come out very sticky and resistant — not at all runny.

51

GOOD ENOUGH FOR 300,000?

Parents, has your child ever asked you to make their favorite food for a school-wide function? Brittany, our middle daughter of three and a student at the University of Georgia at the time, did — boy-oh-boy did she! She was to submit her favorite recipe for UGA annual campus-wide Thanksgiving dinner for over 20,000 students, faculty, staff, and alumni.

Perhaps you're unfamiliar with some of the outstanding attributes of this illustrious university. UGA was founded in 1785, which makes it the country's oldest state-chartered university. Another accolade is it being the birthplace of the American system of public higher education.

If you're a mathematician or a statistician, you may be impressed with these numbers. UGA's current enrollment is 27,951 students on a 767-acre campus. Their endowment is a whopping 1.017 billion dollars. Britt is now one of over 300,000 alumni around the world. Also, they usually have a pretty good football team (Go Dawgs!). Considering they have such a vast alumni base, a bulldog graduate never has to "bark alone" on a fall Saturday afternoon as the Dawgs defend their turf between the hedges.

I mentioned that for you to better appreciate the significance of this particular recipe. I realize that some of you are connoisseurs. I am not. I do not love cooking. In fact, I do not even enjoy cooking, although I love to eat great tasting food.

Only once in my life have I prepared a meal for someone else. At the time I was a bachelor who wanted to impress my date with a home-cooked meal. It was a five-course Stouffer's frozen dinner, which I burned. I mean really burnt it…severely.

Needless to say, I am not a good cook; but my wife, Sandra is an excellent cook. One evening Britt called home and asked, "Mom, would you be willing to send a recipe for the UGA Annual

Thanksgiving Dinner and their UGA Alumni Cookbook?"

Sandra, like most people who are talented in a particular skill, initially responded, "Honey, I really don't feel that I am that good." The thought of 300,000 alumni evaluating her recipe was intimidating. However, this was her daughter's request so she said, "Yes, I will do it for you."

The catch was, only four recipes (one per category) out of hundreds submitted, would be selected for the annual UGA Thanksgiving dinner for students, faculty, staff, and alumni.

A month or so later, Sandra received a letter and a commemorative plate recognizing her recipe as being the "Best of the Best" in her category.

Without further ado here is Sandra Gault Keep It Moist's award-winning recipe for Southern Pineapple Casserole.

Tommy and Sandra Gilmore

SOUTHERN PINEAPPLE CASSEROLE

Tommy and Sandra Gilmore

Ingredients

1 20-ounce can pineapple chunks, drained

1 cup sugar

3 tablespoons flour

1 cup grated sharp cheddar cheese

1 stick butter or margarine

1 sleeve Ritz Crackers

Directions

Preheat oven to 350.

1. Pour pineapple into a 1.5-quart baking dish.
2. Mix together sugar, flour, and shredded cheese. Spread over pineapple.
3. Melt 1 stick of butter or margarine in bowl.
4. Crumble a sleeve of Ritz crackers and pour into melted butter. Gently mix.
5. Spread Ritz mixture on top of flour/cheese mixture.
6. Bake 25 minutes at 350°.

Bon Appétit!

52

WHISTLE FOR FLIES

In that day the LORD will whistle for flies from the distant streams of Egypt

and for the bees from the land of Assyria.

Isaiah 7:18 NIV

The fly knew he had the upper hand. He had strategically landed on the counter among all the food items that would eventually evolve into dinner for my family. He knew I couldn't reach him with my dishtowel without knocking everything to the floor. So I stared at him. And he stared back. It was a standoff.

"I'm sick of these flies," my husband said, shooing the fly as he entered the kitchen.

"Just open the screen to the dining room window," I replied.

"And how's that going to help?"

"For whatever reason, the flies come in through the back door and make a straight line for the dining room. If you leave the screen open, they usually find their way out," I said with great authority.

"Well, wouldn't it make sense if we just put the screen back in the kitchen doorway?"

"Yes, it would."

"Where is it?"

"In the garage where you took it. You said you were going to fix the hole in the screen."

He paused. "We have extra screening so I can fix it, right?"

"Yes. You bought extra screening a long time ago. It's somewhere in the garage."

My husband exited the house and headed for the garage. But my attention was still on this fly. My husband had shooed him away from the food, but the fly continued to circle, waiting to come in for a landing. I swatted and swatted at him but only managed to create a nice breeze in the kitchen. The fly taunted me as I continued to miss.

I stopped swinging, waiting for him to land again, and I wondered during this interim why God even bothered to make flies. They serve no useful purpose that I was aware of. Oh, maybe flies were the occasional dinner for birds or for spiders; but beyond that, I questioned why God would make such a nasty vile creature.

Then I recalled that flies were one of the 10 plagues that God sent to Egypt when the Pharaoh refused to let the Israelites go. Flies were the 4th punishment on the Egyptians because of their sin. But this was not the first time flies were equated with sin in the Bible. In a recent Bible reading of mine Isaiah told how God had threatened to bring flies upon the Israelites if they didn't turn from their sin.

Even though the Bible doesn't say when flies were created — whether in the beginning or sometime after the fall of Adam and Eve — I decided that flies would be a reminder of my own sin. If I leave the screen off the window of my door, flies/sin come flying in. If I put the screen back in and it has a hole in it, flies/sin finds its way in. I can even take a few steps back with this analogy and say that if I don't keep things in order, if I don't keep my garage/life clean, I can't fix my screen to prevent flies/sin from coming in. Regardless of how they come in, I know I must not let them stay. I must swat, swing, shoo, spray, and even open other windows — whatever it takes to remove the unwanted guests.

I turned my attention from the fly and to the back door when I saw my husband coming out of the garage. He had found the mesh and had repaired the screen. And as he snapped it back in place, I returned to fixing dinner since I had ushered the first fly out the dining room window. My husband entered the house and proudly ginned at me — he could finally scratch this item off his to-do list. I thanked him but didn't have the heart to tell him another fly had entered when he came in the back door.

PRAYER: Lord, everything you make has a purpose. Let your flies be a reminder for me to deal with the sin that comes into my home and my life. In Jesus' name I pray. Amen.

Lori Marett

SHOO FLY PIE

Lori Marett

Shoofly Pie is also known as Shoo Fly Pie, Shoo-fly Pie, Shoe Fly Pie. There are various thoughts on the origin of the pie itself and its name, however there seems to be agreement on it being a sticky, gooey molasses pie (perhaps named for Shoofly Molasses)

Considering my experiences, I find this a fitting recipe and tend to agree the name likely came from the cooks, upon cooling this sweet pie on the window sill, had to "shoo" the flies away.

Ingredients

¾ cup molasses

¾ cup boiling water

½ teaspoon baking soda

1 single crust pie pastry, rolled flat and placed in a 9-inch pie plate

1½ cups flour

½ cup dark brown sugar

1 teaspoon cinnamon

½ teaspoon nutmeg

⅛ teaspoon salt

¼ pound (1 stick) cold unsalted butter

Directions

Preheat oven to 450°.

1. In a bowl, combine molasses, water and baking soda.
2. Pour into pastry shell.
3. Make the crumb topping by mixing flour, brown sugar, cinnamon, nutmeg and salt together in a bowl. Cut in the butter with a pastry cutter until the consistency resembles cornmeal.
4. Spoon the crumb mixture evenly over the top of the molasses mixture in the shell.
5. Bake 15 minutes at 450° then lower the heat to 350°and bake 20 minutes longer, or until set and firm.

Keep the flyswatter nearby.

53

What's in Your Turkey?

Our second Thanksgiving as a married couple was a big day for me. I'd always loved to cook and finally got the opportunity to share my prowess in the kitchen. This was the early 80s. There were no cooking channels or cooking blogs yet. We only had cookbooks, women's magazines and good old recipe swapping between family and friends.

Unlike many of my friends who hated to cook and nearly broke out in hives at the thought, I didn't have any fears in the kitchen. I loved cooking for other people. I still do. So, this holiday brought the chance to cook my first big holiday meal for our parents and my grandma.

From memory, I made the menu from all of my family favorites. I quizzed my husband, Larry, for his family's special dishes as well. I had it all set. I shopped a couple of times that week making sure I would have everything.

My memory replayed the early morning rising of my mom to get the turkey rinsed and put into the oven for our midday mealtime. I'd never actually gotten up to help with that, but I remembered hearing all the noise down the hall. I recalled her making the stuffing first to be able to put it in the turkey. I did the same. The onions, celery and carrots chopped small and sautéed with the butter. The stock heated to add to the breadcrumbs, too.

At this point, I need to fill you in on a minor detail. I don't like turkey. Really any meat, but turkey by far grosses me out the most. Don't like the smell, don't like the texture — and have you seen what those things look like? So wrestling with this big ugly bird's body early in the morning was, well, let's just say it was more than likely the quickest turkey rinse in history.

The turkey was rinsed off well, out of the sink, patted dry and into the big blue speckled roaster. Check.

Butter smeared all over its body. Ack. Check.

I placed the lid on the roaster and proudly inserted that big bird in the preheated oven. Thrilled with my accomplishment, I went on to set the table. I prepped some of the other dishes being careful not to wake Larry, but apparently the smells were making their way throughout the house.

He joined me in the kitchen and asked if he could help, especially if I needed a taste tester, all the while eyeballing the pecan pie waiting to go in the oven. As I showed him the food that was already completed and those dishes in process, my heart began to fill with joy. I was so excited to be cooking for our family and serving them this meal in our home. This was bliss.

You could smell the home-canned half runner beans simmering in bacon grease. Grandma's famous dinner rolls were squeezed in beside the roasting pan in the oven and caused us all to salivate at the whiff of them. You couldn't help noticing the pecan pie now fighting with the turkey for a part of that olfactory explosion, too. If I close my eyes and think real hard, I might be able to smell it, even now.

The sweet tea was now poured. Our family had chosen seats around the table and eyed the goods. All said how eager they were to dig in. In all honesty, I thought the smells were amazing as well. I could hardly contain myself. I was so excited at how everything looked, smelled and had finished at the appropriate times. The oohs and ahhs of the family weren't too bad either.

Larry helped me get the turkey out of the big roaster and onto a platter. I remember that bird weighing over twenty pounds — I had no idea what size I would need. But, twenty pounds sounded fine for seven of us. Wait, one of us wouldn't be eating it, so that would be twenty pounds for six folks total. That was a lot of turkey.

I sat down at the table last and Larry picked up the large carving set we had received as a wedding gift. He was eager to try it out.

But my mom quickly interjected, "Wait, did you stuff it, Tammy?"

"Yes, both ends like you said," I said.

"Well, Larry, you'll wanna empty those first. It's easier to get out now."

I passed Larry the serving bowl set aside for the stuffing so he could empty out the two areas. He pulled the stuffing out of the, ahem, lower end. He turned the turkey around to remove stuffing from the neck area.

"This end didn't get much stuffing. There wasn't much room to put anything in there. I don't even know why anyone bothers," I said.

My mom and grandma looked at me, then each other.

At this point, Larry pulled out this gnarly looking hook-shaped thing.

"Eew, what is that?" I winced.

My father-in-law chuckled and said, "Oh yeah, that's the neck, I'll take that."

I have to say that at this point the desire to even try my own turkey was beginning to fade. I had been trying to talk myself into it, but now, uh…maybe not.

And then…

"Oh look," Larry said. I glanced back to see Larry holding a bag of something.

"What is that?" I said.

"The liver and gizzards bag," he said.

My jaw dropped. I said, "The *what*?"

The entire table began to snicker then one by one they all just gave in and burst into a hearty chuckle, creating a loud chorus of laughter. I decided then and there I would not be eating this thing.

Nobody else was fazed by it and all were kind in saying the turkey turned out very good and moist, just like a turkey should be.

So they said. I wouldn't know.

So, if you are making your first turkey this year for your family, take it from someone who truly knows a bit about turkey making now. When you rinse that big bird and get it ready for roasting, be sure to reach into that neck cavity — gulp — and remove those extra parts that are shoved in there. Unless of course it is your plan all along to keep the conversation lively at the family holiday dinner table.

Tammy Karasek

CHICKEN (OR TURKEY!) POT PIE

Tammy Karasek

Ingredients

3-4 large chicken breasts
5-6 small redskin potatoes
(not peeled)
3 carrots, chopped bite-sized
1 large onion, chopped
1 8-ounce container of sour
cream

1 cup (or more) shredded
cheddar cheese
1 can cream of chicken soup
salt and pepper to taste
1 package of 2 Pillsbury pie
crusts
1 tablespoon melted butter

Directions

It looks like a lot of steps, but read through recipe before beginning, it's not that bad!

Preheat oven to 375°.

1. Boil chicken until done, approximately 25-30 minutes. Remove from water and shred.

2. Boil potatoes, carrots and onions together until soft (but not mushy) and drain.

3. In large bowl, place shredded chicken, cooked vegetables, sour cream, shredded cheddar, cream of chicken soup and about 1 teaspoon of salt and ½ teaspoon of pepper. (If you like things with a little more salt or pepper or even without any, adjust the amounts.)

4. Mix all of the ingredients well.

5. Place one of the crusts in the bottom of a large pie dish.

6. Add pie filling and spread out.

7. Top with other piecrust and vent by making slices in top crust. (I like using mini cookie cutters matching the season or hearts if I'm delivering it to someone. Use cutter

to make the hole first, then place the crust on top of the mixture and place the piece that was removed decoratively on the top.)

8. Trim off any extra crust if you have it and crimp edges.

9. Brush top crust with the butter.

10. Bake at 375° until brown and bubbly, about 45 minutes.

11. Let sit about ten minutes before serving so it sets up a bit. (Although my family has never allowed that to happen.)

Variation: You can use the leftover turkey from Thanksgiving and use the same ingredients. Although I changed it up for the family by using cream of celery soup instead of the chicken soup!

Leftover piecrust trimmings and melted butter? Roll the crust flat, brush with the leftover butter and sprinkle a little bit of sugar all over it. Bake in the same 375° oven about 15-20 minutes, watching it until it's golden…a little snack for those kitchen snoopers that are sure to come through once this is baking. Or keep it for yourself. I'm not telling.

54

SALT OR LIGHT

As a little girl, I was very much a Papa's girl. There was nothing like spending a few days with my grandparents.

Often when I visited, we found ourselves in the kitchen, cooking. Papa was a cook in the Army during World War II and was a wonderful cook. I don't remember a lot of his dishes, but one vividly remains in my memory. That is the peach cobbler he made from scratch.

One evening in my early teen years, I decided to cook a dessert for the family. However, I did not have the recipe in front of me. I was recreating the recipe by remembering what Papa had done.

First, the flour went in. Then I prepared the peaches and poured the milk. Looking at the ingredients I had gathered on the counter, I realized I was forgetting something. But what was it? I scratched my head and thought for a moment.

Then I walked to the cabinet, picked up the missing item and poured a cup of the white substance into the measuring cup, proud of myself for the dish I'd made. After the family finished the evening meal, I presented the peace cobbler I'd cooked.

After his first bite, Daddy laid down his spoon and took a long sip of milk. Finally he asked, "Um…what did you put in here?"

"Well, flour, peaches, salt and milk," I answered proudly. Then I took my first bite. There was a very strange taste in my mouth. Something wasn't right. This didn't taste the way Papa's peach cobbler tasted.

"Are you sure you were supposed to put salt?" Daddy pushed his plate away.

"Of course. Wasn't I?" I thought hard. Had I made a mistake? After all, this clearly wasn't Papa's cobbler.

Daddy said, "I think it was supposed to be sugar."

I clasped a hand over my mouth at Daddy's pronouncement.

I had made a mistake and substituted salt for sugar. That substitution had changed the texture and taste of the cobbler, making inedible what should have been a delectable dessert.

All of my hard work went into the trash and I was embarrassed by my mistake. A vital ingredient was worthless when substituted by another.

On Sunday, Daddy stood in the pulpit and read Matthew 5:13 NLT: *"You are the salt of the earth. But what good is salt if it has lost its flavor? Can you make it useful again? It will be thrown out and trampled underfoot as worthless."*

He stopped reading and began to talk about salt and its purpose. Then he told the story of my faux pas earlier that week. I squirmed in my seat, embarrassed by my mistake.

Daddy continued to read, picking up where he had left off on the fourteenth verse. *"You are the light of the world — like a city on a mountain, glowing in the night for all to see. Don't hide your light under a basket! Instead, put it on a stand and let it shine for all. In the same way, let your good deeds shine out for all to see, so that everyone will praise your heavenly Father."*

He ended his sermon by asking, "Do you want to be the salt of the earth and trampled underfoot? Or do you want to be the salt of the world and bring glory to your Father in heaven?"

Others seemed to think my incident with the peach cobbler was a delightful conversation piece. Later on, I too could laugh about it. Daddy was able to use that to make valid points in a sermon. As a result, I never forgot those points.

My switching salt for sugar changed the texture of the peach cobbler. In life, it's the opposite. No matter how sweet we might be, the Lord tells us to be salt in this world, giving flavor and spice to others, and bringing glory to God in how we live.

Now, every time I add sugar to a recipe, it pops into my mind, "Sugar in here, salt out there in the world!"

Diana Leagh Matthews

55

GLORIA'S GARLIC-KY TACOS

My sister and her husband surprised me with a visit one Saturday morning. We drew up an action plan and out the door we went. Our fun day included shopping, ice-skating, and eating a delicious brunch.

Back at my house later, hours passed as we reminisced with storytelling, laughing, and drinking pots of coffee.

We were having such a great time, we didn't want it to end, but noticing the setting sun, my sister said they'd better not wear out their welcome, and get on the road.

"Not without supper," I said, "I have hamburger meat in the fridge. I can whip up some tasty tacos in a few minutes." After all, that would be better than stopping at a drive-thru on their way home.

They agreed to stay and eat with me. My sister offered to help cook but I told her I'd rather she and her husband sit in the dining area next to the galley kitchen. We could still talk and see each other while I cooked.

They took a seat and relaxed and I began my preparations. When I make tacos, I begin by following the seasoning packet directions, and then enhance that by adding onions.

When the meat is almost ready, I add garlic. As the meat began to brown, the aroma of seasoning and onions increased our appetites. I took the garlic powder container from the spice rack, unscrewed the top and laid it aside. There's no need to measure something I'm accustomed to doing, like shaking salt, pepper, or garlic onto taco mix. So I continued to talk, looking at my family more than looking at the skillet of taco meat.

I looked down into the skillet to stir, and gasped, "Oh, no!" A heaping hill of garlic powder sat smack in the center of my taco meat! The garlic shaker was empty. My eyes widened and by then my sister, with open mouth, was staring at what I'd done.

I scooped the white garlic powder out of the meat by spoonsful onto a separate plate. My sister's husband said, "I was wondering if you meant to put that much garlic in there. But—" he added quickly. "I really like garlic."

I gave him a look. Maybe he was trying to make me not feel embarrassed. But it sounded a lot like what I'd heard people say before, when they mention something a person cooked and quickly add, "…but that's the way I like it."

I managed a feeble laugh. "Good thing you like garlic. These will be the best you've ever had."

I looked at the garlic shaker and saw what had happened. The top with shaker holes was not on the container. So, instead of sprinkling, I was dumping garlic into the skillet.

In hard shells, combined with all the fixin's, we all agreed dinner wasn't too bad for a quick meal… although I have to confess, less garlic is better.

We had a good laugh that day (and even for years later!) about Gloria's Garlic-ky Tacos.

Gloria Spears

Gloria's Not-So-Garlicky Tacos

Gloria Spears

Ingredients for filling

1 pound ground meat

1 packet taco seasoning

chopped onion (to taste)

garlic powder (to taste)

Directions

1. Brown meat.

2. Add taco seasoning and chopped onions.

3. Continue cooking following directions on taco seasoning packet.

4. When meat is almost done, sprinkle in (don't dump) garlic to taste.

Make available

taco shells

salsa

lettuce

tomato

cheese

sour cream

56

THE ATTACK
OF THE KILLER TAMALES

From my early childhood I recall my dad as a kind and considerate man, especially toward Mom. That was not always the case, according to my Uncle Ted. Early in their marriage, Dad tended to ignore Mom. His stubbornness and impatience were the cause of many serious arguments.

Dad changed after what my Uncle Ted called, "The Attack of the Killer Tamales." Whenever he told the story he would begin with a chuckle. By the time he finished, the room would be filled with his deep, bass laughter.

One day, Mom was in the kitchen making preparations for lunch. She was heating a can of tamales by placing it in a pan of water. She put the pan on the stove and turned the burner on high just as Dad and Uncle Ted walked in and sat at the kitchen table. Dad was carrying his Colt 45 pistol. He laid it on the table along with the cleaning materials. The sound attracted Mom's attention. She was immediately upset when she saw the gun.

"No!" she said firmly to my dad. "You take that stuff out into the garage. I told you before, I don't want that gun in this house. It's dangerous. We have two small boys. Get it and everything that goes with it out of my kitchen. Now!"

Dad didn't even look up. He ignored her as usual. Because of the distraction over the issue of the gun, Mom was unaware that the pan of water containing the tamales had started boiling. Even worse, she had forgotten to punch a hole in the top of the can to keep pressure from building up as the contents heated.

Uncle Ted said to my dad, "I think she's right. We should move all this out to the garage."

Dad chose to disregard Uncle Ted's advice. He maintained his silence and began arranging his cleaning tools.

Mom left the stove and walked up behind Dad. "I've had enough," she said. "When I tell you I will not tolerate having weapons in the house around our little boys, I mean it." She reached over his shoulder, grabbed his pistol and stepped back to the kitchen door.

At that same moment, the can of tamales exploded with a loud "Pow!" The contents flew across the room, hitting Dad in the back of his head. He grabbed his neck with both hands. When he saw the dripping dark, red-colored mush he was holding, his eyes and mouth flew open.

"He tried to speak, but before he could utter a word, he fainted. Your dad was fine when he recovered a few minutes later," Uncle Ted assured me, while laughing. "But by the look on your dad's face, I knew he thought your mom shot him and blew his brains out."

Uncle Ted loved telling this story. "Your dad's personality changed overnight after those tamales hit him," he said. "He started paying more attention to your mom. He sought her opinions and ideas, and actually listened. Disagreements were few and far between."

It's still difficult for me to imagine my dad being anything but kind and considerate. It's amazing what can be accomplished with a can of exploding tamales.

Robert W. Rettie

57

WHEN LIFE
GIVES YOU LEMONS

It was my first attempt to bake a pie, so I didn't realize what a challenge I was taking on. I was twelve years old and required to bake a pie for a 4-H project. *Lemon Meringue*, I thought. I'll surprise mother and serve it for her picnic next week.

I assembled all of the ingredients and carefully studied the recipe. First the crust. When I rolled it out, it tore apart. What to do?

Maybe more butter. Carefully, I cut the additional butter into the dough with two table knives. It rolled out better, but it still wasn't big enough to cover the pan.

More butter?

I added more butter. That worked! Now to the filling.

My mouth could already feel the tartness of the lemons as I prepared the mixture. I put it on the stove to thicken, then stirred and stirred. It got somewhat thicker, but was still runny.

Maybe it will thicken while it is in the oven.

While the crust and filling baked, I combined sugar and egg whites to make the meringue. After taking the hot mixture from the oven, I topped it with the whipped egg whites that stood in firm peaks. My pie would be a success!

But...when at the picnic and I cut into the pie, the filling ran over the edges of the pie pan and I had to dip with a spoon to serve.

"What did I do wrong?" I asked Mother and we discussed the ingredients. She questioned my mention of corn syrup.

I remembered a substitute. "Well," I said. "The recipe called for corn...something, and the only corn thing I saw in the cabinet was corn syrup. You weren't here to ask, so I used the corn syrup."

She nicely pointed out that corn starch, not corn syrup, is for thickening.

I was pleased when people complimented me on the flavor of the pie. However, I was quickly deflated when someone asked, "Does anyone have a straw?"

As the years progressed I continued in my quest to make the perfect lemon pie. Whoever said, "Easy as pie" didn't mean lemon meringue. Some pies may be easy, but this one is a challenge. It's actually like making three separate things — crust, filling, and topping. Any one of them can go wrong.

In high school Home Economics class I learned that when you are making the filling you must *always* add the hot mixture to the eggs, not the other way around. Otherwise, the result is a curdled mess.

By the time I was out of college I was engaged and still living at home. My fiancé, Dave, found the last piece of my lemon pie in mother's refrigerator. We struggled over that piece of pie, both of us wanting it. Alas, the dish fell to the floor, breaking into a myriad of pieces and splattering the pie everywhere.

When Dave and I moved to Mesa, Arizona, our next-door neighbors had a lemon tree! They developed the habit of dropping a bag of ripe lemons on our doorstep. That was my cue to bake them a lemon pie.

One day when a friend and her mother came to visit I gave them a lemon pie to take home to their family. Sometime later they phoned and said, "We ate the whole pie in the car. The family didn't get so much as one bite!"

Another time I took a pie to a potluck dinner at our church. Stepping out of line, Dave put a note on the pie. "Don't eat this pie! It's bad for you!" Predictably, there were only a few crumbs in the pie plate when it was Dave's turn to serve himself.

As years went by, I continued my quest for the perfect lemon meringue pie. I tried new recipes. Some people put the lemon juice in the filling before they cook it. Others insist upon adding the juice after the filling is cooked.

I experimented and realized that the second method resulted

in my preference — a tart filling that melts in the mouth when taking a bite of all three layers of the pie.

A friend took issue with me, saying her pie was better because she used the first method. I made a pie and boldly delivered it to her door. Unfortunately, I lost a friend over that experience, and I regret it to this day.

The adage goes, "When life gives you lemons, make lemonade." I say, "When life gives you lemons, make lemon meringue pie!"

Mary Ellen Weber

58

Are You Hungry or Just Eating?

Blessed are those who hunger and thirst for righteousness,
for they shall be filled.

Matthew 5:6 NKJV

I was enjoying breakfast this morning when God showed up. Halfway through my store-brand yogurt mixed with fresh blueberries, he floated a question across my mind. "Are you hungry?" When I replied, "Of course I'm hungry; that's why I'm having breakfast," he floored me with, "No, are you truly hungry or are you just eating?" That's when our discussion morphed into a monologue and I tried keeping up.

Usually when we're not really hungry, we approach food as optional. We develop a choosy, disinterested mindset. Then, if we do find something to eat, we pick at it and often leave leftovers behind.

By comparison, a truly hungry or starving person has no doubt about his hunger. *He has to eat!* Hunger pangs make him very intentional. Then, when he finds a food source, he devours it. He may even eat things that normally wouldn't be his top menu selections and eat them at places he never thought he would go. Oddly enough, only food satisfies a truly hungry person.

Yes, real hunger makes us behave in strange, yet passionate and intentional ways.

Okay, now back to my conversation with God. Jesus said those who hunger and thirst for righteousness would be filled. But the secret is in truly hungering for it, not merely picking and choosing as we aimlessly wander up and down his spiritual buffet. Nothing else quenches our craving; our appetite is only for him and his delicacies.

When I genuinely hunger for him and his righteousness, my attitude and actions change. I prioritize specific time with him. I crave his insight, conviction, and direction. I readily devour even those things he offers that I normally wouldn't accept. Like David, my heart will pant for him. Like Mary, I will desire sitting in his presence. Like Paul, I will set my affections on things above. Like Jesus, I will lovingly invite others to his feast.

PRAYER: Oh, God, never let me settle for the unhealthy fast food of the world and its alluring distractions. Give me spiritual hunger pangs that drive me to the banquet hall of your Word. Grant me the intentional desire to feast in your presence. Please quench my insatiable hunger with only yourself.

Nate Stevens

* * *

I am the bread of life.
No one who comes to me will ever be hungry again....
I am the true bread from heaven.
Jesus
John 6:35, 51 NLT

* * *

Blessed are those who hunger and thirst for righteousness,
For they shall be filled.
Matthew 5:6 NKJV

About the Authors

Ellen Andersen grew up in California and has lived in Greenville, South Carolina since 2002. She loves to garden. Ellen serves in her church as a Stephen Minister. She can relate to and minister to others who are hurting since she deals with ongoing physical issues of her own. Ellen has published several devotions online at christiandevotioins.us. Connect with her at www.ellenandersen.blogspot.com or on Twitter at @EllenAndersenSC.

Carol A. Baird is a member of The Volusia County Chapter of Word Weavers. She worked in the corporate world, writing business letters and procedure manuals. For eleven years, she taught a lunchtime adult Bible study class at The Travelers in Hartford, Connecticut. She researched, wrote the lessons, and compiled them in book format for teaching. After retiring, she served as a church treasurer, leader of an evangelism team, and Bible study leader. Varied in her creativity, Carol plays a console Hammond organ, has written 20+ songs, does paper craft, and constructs personalized greeting cards. In the past three years she has written 150 poems that are categorized: (1) My Legacy for Family and Friends; (2) Storytelling through Rhyme; (3) Rare and Beautiful Treasurers; and (4) Reflections. She has not considered publishing until now.

Carolyn Roth Barnum coordinates "Write People," a writer's group at Wesley Village Retirement Community in Wilmore, Kentucky where she has resided the past five years since moving from Jackson, Michigan. Other than two stories previously published in the Moments series (*Precious, Precocious Moments* and *Additional Christmas Moments*), her articles have appeared in *Woman's World* and *Reminisce* magazines. During her career she held various secretarial and administrative assistant positions including Michigan District of Kiwanis where she helped plan and coordinate state and international conventions. She enjoys writing, reading and spending time with her daughters, Laura and Nancy, who live in nearby Lexington.

Janet Beagle, PhD is a writer, speaker, and student of God's word. In addition to blogging "tiny seeds of Christian reflection," her writing has appeared in Focus on the Family's *Clubhouse* magazine, *The Secret*

Place, The Word in Season, and others. She also serves as the director of graduate programs for Purdue University's College of Engineering. In her spare time, she likes to eat other people's cooking and hike with her dog, Marly. Visit Janet at www.mustardpatch.org.

AimeeAnn Blythe is a freelance writer, published author, and is currently working on ideas for books in three different genres. Her two furry children are by her "creative" side every step of the way. info@aimeeannblythe.com

Mason K Brown is a freelance author and storyteller of inspirational non-fiction and humor. Her work is published in seven volumes of the *Chicken Soup for the Soul* collection; *Guideposts*; *RAIN Magazine* 2013, 2014, 2015 and 2016; *Help! I'm a Parent* (7 contributions); *When God Makes Lemonade*; *Precious, Precocious Moments*; *Seeds of...an anthology of Pacific Northwest writers Volumes I and II*; *More Christmas Moments*; *The Mother's Heart Magazine*; *Abba's Promises*; *Vista* (12 times); *The Secret Place* (13 times) and others. She was a finalist in the 2016 Cascade Writers Contest, published devotional division.

Rob Buck is a business owner who ministers to men in the work place. He is husband to Betsy, his bride of 36 years, is father of four and grandfather of six. He's an elder at Columbia Crossroads Church in Columbia, South Carolina. Rob is president of Alpha Training and Services, an IT training company and treasurer of Focused Living, www.focusedliving.com. Rob enjoys gardening, chicken farming and pool. He also plays disc golf and has built an 18-hole course on his property. Rob is a member of Word Weavers International. His writings have been published in several magazines and newspapers including *Christian Standard, Columbia Star* and *Reach Out Columbia*. Rob's first novel, *Beyond Time*, was published by Oak Tara. The sequel, *Home Remains*, was published in 2017. He regularly posts to his blog www.joy-in-the-journey.com.

Penelope Carleveto is British born and an avid tea lover. She grew up with tea as a way of life. Author of several books, including *Tea on the Titanic* and *First Class Etiquette*, she is also a speaker on every aspect of tea. She has written numerous articles for magazines and currently writes a column in *Leading Hearts Magazine*, co-hosts Cooking up Wonders, and is noted for her role as the Ambassador of Tea. A passionate traveler,

Penelope leads groups on her annual Taste of Britain tea tour to the British Isles. She and her husband reside in Colorado, have three grown children and are grandparents of 11 future tea lovers.

Rebecca Carpenter writes at her lake retreat near Orlando. After retiring from teaching elementary school, she and her husband traveled the world for missions and pleasure. Experiences with her granddaughters, traveling, and nature inspire her writings. Her articles have appeared in Focus on the Family's *Clubhouse* and *Clubhouse Jr.* magazines, *Christmas Moments, Merry Christmas Moments,* and *Loving Moments.* After losing her husband and both parents within months she wrote page after page of her grief journey. Forty of these devotions are in her book, *Ambushed by Glory in My Grief.* Visit her at http://rebeccacarpenter.blogspot.com.

Lauren Craft believes our Heavenly Father gives each of his children a purpose, and fulfilling his plan is one of the greatest joys we can experience before reaching our eternal home. In addition to writing, God has blessed Lauren with opportunities to aid in Bible translation and share the gospel on four continents. You can connect with her at www.laurencraftauthor.com.

Jessica H. Crowell is passionate for Christ and getting the message of the Gospel out through her Facebook page, Coffee with Jesse. She lives in Fyffe, Alabama with her beloved husband Kevin, aka Cowboy, and her two sons Kyle and Hunter, along with the two canines Shorty and Copper who rule the roost. She loves meeting with God on a daily basis in her secret garden, which is not so secret, now that she posts videos of how God not only works in her life, but how he will also work in yours.

Lola Di Giulio De Maci is a retired teacher whose stories have appeared in numerous editions of *Chicken Soup for the Soul, Los Angeles Times, Sasee,* and *Reminisce* magazines, as well as children's publications. Lola has a Master of Arts in education and English. She writes overlooking the San Bernardino Mountains. You may contact her at LDeMaci@aol.com.

Diana Derringer is an award-winning writer and author of *Beyond Bethlehem and Calvary: 12 Dramas for Christmas, Easter, and More!* She enjoys traveling with her husband and serving as a friendship family to international university students. Her blog, www.dianaderringer.com, helps people with a non-English background understand the meaning of unusual English expressions and offers a brief respite for anyone who enjoys word play.

Terri Elders received her first byline in 1946 on a piece about how bats saved her family's home from fire, published on the children's page of the *Portland Oregonian*. At nine years old, she hadn't known that her title, "Bats in Our Belfry," would lead readers to suspect her family's sanity. Her stories have appeared in over 100 anthologies. She can be contacted at telders@hotmail.com.

Karen Friday is a pastor's wife and women's ministry leader. She's an award-winning writer and avid speaker who loves words and God's Word. Karen earned a communications degree and has experience in a broad spectrum of business services where she is frequently referred to as Girl Friday. A blogger, Karen "Girl" Friday engages a community every week. *Hope is Among Us* is an award-winning blog that expresses scriptural truths as life happens. Karen has published a number of articles and devotions in both print and online media and writes as a regular contributor for the national site, *Inspire a Fire*. She is currently working on her first book project about God's goodness and mercy. Karen and her husband Mike reside in Johnson City, Tennessee and have two grown children and a grandson. The entire family is fond of the expression, "TGIF: Thank God it's Friday." They owe Monday an apology.

Tommy Scott Gilmore, III is a Christian motivational speaker and Executive Director of Changing Lives Ministry of Asheville, North Carolina (http://www.changinglivesministry.info/). He is a graduate of Taylor University and Gordon Conwell Theological Seminary having earned a B.S. and Master's Degree in Education. He is published in *Decision Magazine, The Christian Athlete, The National Network of Youth Ministries, Single Minded,* and *WNC Parent.* While serving as Pastor to Students and Families, he had numerous articles published in the popular *Youth Specialties Encyclopedia for Youth Workers.* He also wrote a supplemental Bible study in conjunction with Steven Curtis Chapman's *For The Sake of the Call.* He has written two training manuals: *Changing Lives Training Manual for Youth Workers* and *The Comprehensive Pro-Life Manual.* Tommy has contributed articles to eight *Divine Moments* books. Other than talking to his best friend, Jesus, Tommy enjoys chillin' with his beautiful wife of 30+ years, Sandra, his 3 grown daughters (Lindsey, Brittany and Meghan) son-in-law (Brian), his two granddaughters (Sarah and Victoria), and two best buddies, whose tails never stop wagging, Mr. Finnegan and Kirby or "Special K."

Lydia E. Harris has been married to her college sweetheart, Milt, for fifty years. They have two married children and five grandchildren ranging in age from seven to eighteen. Lydia earned a Master of Arts degree in home economics. She has written numerous articles, book reviews, devotionals, and stories. Focus on the Family's *Clubhouse* magazines for children publish her recipes, which she develops and tests with her grandchildren. She writes the column, "A Cup of Tea with Lydia," and is called "Grandma Tea" by her grandchildren. Lydia has contributed to numerous books and is author of the book, *Preparing My Heart for Grandparenting: For Grandparents at Any Stage of the Journey.*

Helen L. Hoover and her husband are retired and live in Northwest Arkansas. Sewing, reading, knitting, traveling, and helping her husband with home repair occupy her time. Word Aflame Publishing, *The Secret Place, Word Action Publication, The Quiet Hour, The Lutheran Digest,* Light and Life Communications, *Chicken Soup for the Soul,* and *Victory in Grace* have published her devotionals and personal articles. Visits with their two living children, grandchildren and great-grandchildren are treasured.

Tammy Karasek sees humor and causes laughter in every aspect of life, then shares about them on her blog. Tammy's past, filled with bullying and criticism from family, is the driving force of her passion to always encourage others and give them a reason to smile. She is a Christian who is blissfully wedded to her college sweetheart, Larry, for 36+ years, is mom to their grown daughter, Kristen and is wrapped around the paw of a little puppy named Hattie. Connect with Tammy at http://www.tammykarasek.com. Contact her at tickledpinktammy@gmail.com

Alice Klies has written since she could hold a pencil. She is currently president of Northern Arizona Word Weavers, a chapter of an international writers group. Through their encouragement Alice began to submit her work for publication. She has nonfiction and fiction stories published in seventeen anthologies. She is a seven-time contributor to *Chicken Soup for the Soul* books and has articles published in *Angels On Earth, AARP* and *Wordsmith Journal.* She has been featured in the

Women of Distinction magazine. Alice's novel, *Pebbles in My Way*, based on her testimony, was released in September 2017 by Little Cab Press. In addition to her involvement in Word Weavers, she is a deaconess and Stephens Minister in her church. Alice is a retired teacher who resides with her husband and two Golden Retrievers in beautiful Cottonwood, Arizona. She prays her stories cause a reader to smile, laugh or cry, and most of all turn their eyes to God who loves them.

Nancy Julien Kopp is a Kansan, originally from Chicago but has lived in the Flint Hills of Kansas for many years. She writes creative nonfiction, memoir, inspirational, award-winning children's fiction, poetry and articles on the writing craft. She's published in eighteen *Chicken Soup for the Soul* books, other anthologies, newspapers, e-zines and internet radio. She blogs about her writing world with tips and encouragement for writers at www.writergrannysworld.blogspot.com.

Barbara Latta is a freelance writer whose passion is to share how the grace of God can free us from the rules of religious tradition. Her articles, devotions, and poems have been published in newspapers, magazines, and websites. She writes a monthly column for the *Pike Journal-Reporter* in Zebulon, Georgia. She is a board member of the East Metro Atlanta Christian Writers. She enjoys riding motorcycles with her Harley husband, and their biker travels are the inspiration for her bog, *Navigating Life's Curves*, at barbaralatta.blogspot.com.

Yvonne Lehman is a best-selling author of 58 novels and compiler of 10 non-fiction books. She founded and directed the Blue Ridge Mountains Christian Writers Conference for 25 years and now directs the Blue Ridge "Autumn in the Mountains" Novelist Retreat held annually in October. She has joined Lighthouse Publishing of the Carolinas as Acquisitions and Managing Editor of Candlelight Romance and Guiding Light Women's Fiction. She earned a Master's Degree in English from Western Carolina University and has taught English and Creative Writing on the college level. Her recent novel releases are a novella *Have Dress Will Marry* (*Heart of a Cowboy* collection), *Better Latte than Never*, and 8 Romances (4 set in South Carolina, 4 set in North Carolina). Her non-fiction *Divine Moments* series is published by Grace Publishing. Released in 2017 were *Merry Christmas Moments* and *The Gift* (*Secret Admirer* collection, Winged Pub). Her 50th novel is *Hearts that Survive – A Novel of the Titanic*, which she signs periodically at the Titanic Museum in Pigeon Forge, Tennessee. She blogs at www.christiansread.com and Novel Rocket. www.yvonnelehman.com. Contact her at yvonnelehman3@gmail.com.

Lori Marett and her husband, Rodney, directed the Gideon Media Arts Conference & Film Festival for several years. Her screenwriting career began two decades ago when she won and/or was finalist for many regional and national screenplay contests, which opened the door for her to adapt producer Ken Wales' *Sea of Glory* for the screen. Her first feature film, *Meant to Be* (co-written with producer/director Bradley Dorsey) was released in 2012. She adapted author Jenny L. Cote's novel, *The Ark, the Reed, and the Fire Cloud* into a screenplay in pre-production for an animated feature film and animated television series. Lori lives in the mountains of western North Carolina. She has written for other *Moments* books.

Diana Leagh Matthews is a vocalist, speaker, writer, life coach, genealogist and a certified Activities Director for a nursing facility. She is a Christian Communicators graduate and has been published in several anthologies, including several *Moments* books. She currently resides in Taylors, South Carolina. Visit her at www.DianaLeaghMatthews. com and www.alookthrutime.com.

Beverly Hill McKinney has published over 300 inspirational articles in such publications as *Good Old Days, Breakthrough Intercessor, Just Between Us, Women Alive, P31,* and *Plus Magazine.* She has devotions in *Cup of Comfort Devotional — Daily Reflections of God's Grace and Love, Open Windows, God Still Meets Needs,* and *God Still Leads and Guides.* Her stories have been featured in anthologies such as *Christmas Miracles, Men of Honor, Guidepost Extraordinary Answers to Prayer, Christian Miracles,* and *Precious, Precocious Moments.* She has also self-published two books, *Through the Parsonage Window* and *Whispers from God, Poems of Inspiration.* She graduated from the Jerry B. Jenkins Christian Writer's Guild and lives in Rogue River, Oregon.

Jaclyn S. Miller is a freelance writer and editor as well as an early childhood educator from northern Indiana. She is a member of SCBWI whose work has been published or awaits publication at *Highlights for Children, Spider, Clubhouse, Clubhouse Jr., Skipping Stones, Kiki, Susie, Encounter, Christian Market,* and in *Chicken Soup for the Soul:*

Campus Chronicles, God Makes Lemonade, and Gryphon House's *Learn Every Day* series.

Vicki H. Moss is Contributing Editor for *Southern Writers Magazine,* a former columnist for *American Daily Herald,* and author of *How to Write for Kids' Magazines* and *Writing with Voice.* She has written for several magazines and was selected to be a presenter of her fiction and creative nonfiction short stories for three consecutive conferences at the Southern Women Writers Conference held at Rome, Georgia's Berry College. Vicki is a speaker and on faculty for writers conferences. For more information about Vicki visit livingwaterfiction.com.

Karen Lynn Nolan is a product of her southern Appalachian heritage of storytelling, mystery, humor, deep faith, and stubborn refusal to give up in the face of overwhelming odds. Her education in fine arts (music, acting, creative writing, and art), survival of natural disasters and misadventures, divorce, financial ruin, and chronic illness fuel her writing mission to give hope to anyone who struggles. Karen's writing credits include stories in anthologies, poetry, newspaper features, blogs, non-profit promotional materials, drama for churches and schools, and commercials/PSAs for Christian radio. Her first novel, set in the Appalachian coalfields, is scheduled for release in November 2018. Karen has won several awards for her writing. She resides in Powder Springs, Georgia and has one awesome adult son. Contact Karen at karenlynnnolan@gmail.com, @KarenlynnNolan on Twitter, or her blog at diamondsinmycoalbucket.blogspot.com

Marilyn Nutter, of Greer, South Carolina is the author of three devotional books and a contributor to magazines, on-line sites and compilations. She is a Bible teacher and speaker for women's groups, a grief support facilitator, and serves on the women's ministry council at her church. Visit marilynnutter.blogspot.com and www.marilynnutter.com. Contact her at marilynnutter@gmail.com

Natalie Ogbourne is fascinated by the roads we wander. A midwest-dwelling wife, mom, and conflicted outdoorsy type, she's perpetually on the hunt for a skirt that will stand up to the trail because she loves the places they take us and all they give to think about along the way. She writes about life's journey, particularly the intersections of actual, everyday life and faith at natalieogbourne.com.

Kim Peterson, as a child, disappeared up her cherry trees with a good book and a thermos of juice. As an adult, her love for the written word is expressed through mentoring aspiring writers online at Taylor University and previously as Associate Faculty in Writing at Bethel College. As a freelance writer, editor, and conference speaker, her writing has appeared in various anthologies, including *Chicken Soup for the Caregiver's Soul* and *Rocking Chair Reader: Family Gatherings.* Her articles and book reviews have been published in local newspapers and in magazines including *Christian Market, Encounter, The Secret Place,* and *Seek,* among others.

Robert (Bob) W. Rettie has always been interested in writing. He has kept journals of his extensive travels and experiences. Born in Selma, California, his father's army career meant growing up in various locations including Luzon in the Philippines. After completing high school, Bob enlisted in the U.S. Navy where he served in the Pacific Submarine Fleet. Taking advantage of the G.I. bill, he graduated from California Fresno State College. A position with the Army and Air Force Exchange Service allowed him to once again travel in the U.S. and abroad including the Republic of South Korea. After retiring, Bob moved to Lexington, Kentucky to be near his son. There he participated in a writing class at the Carnegie Center. Health issues persuaded Bob to seek independent living at Wesley Village Retirement Community located in Wilmore, Kentucky, near Lexington. He joined "Write People" at Wesley Village. Bob shares his humorous writings and memoirs at the Village "Open Mic" nights, likes spending time with friends, and participates in numerous Village activities.

Toni Armstrong Sample retired early to Greenwood, South Carolina at the end of a successful career as a Human Resource Executive, with the final fifteen years as the Owner/President of an HR Consulting and Training firm that she founded. Toni has written for professional journals, recreational magazines, devotionals, newspapers, and inspirational story publications. Her first inspirational romance novel, *The Glass Divider,* was released in 2014 followed by *Transparent Web of Dreams, Distortion,* and *A Still Small Voice.* Two novels, *The Soup Kitchen Gala* and *The Song of My Soul* were released in 2017, along with her first non-fiction book, *I'll Never Be the Same.* Toni is a Christian Retreat leader, conference speaker, Christian Education and Women's Bible Study facilitator. She is a Commission Artist concentrating on the painting of biblical scenes and characters.

Cybele Sieradski, born in Detroit, Michigan now lives in Cottonwood, Arizona. She has lived in 27 homes in 8 states, and has driven 21 cars to and from 47 jobs. When you read that, you might think she is compulsive; but *she* claims she is scattered. While earning a BA in English at Maryville College in Tennessee, she discovered New Directions publications in a bookstore in Knoxville. She aspired to be a Beatnik and write poetry like Ferlinghetti and ee cummings. However, she married a space engineer and brought up her autistic stepson (with amazing success). She acquired an MA in Experimental Psychology and for a few years performed program evaluations for social service agencies. After eons of immersion in technical writing and editing, Cybele has returned to her true passion. Creative energy once more flows. At home in the desert, she cooks and writes poetry, memoir, and essays with relish.

Janet Sobczyk is a substitute teacher by day and an award-winning poet/writer by night. She is married and lives in Omaha, Nebraska. Janet's work has been published in magazines, anthologies, and as guest blog posts. She's a member of the NE Writers Guild and Wordsower's Christian Writers. Her blog of poetry and photos may be found at www.momsmusingsblog.blogspot.com.

Gloria Spears lives in the Tennesse foothills of the Great Smoky Mountains. Gloria has been journaling and writing for enjoyment since her teen years. For many years, she was editor of a resort newsletter in her family business. She now works full time as a realtor locally and in surrounding counties during the day, and writes in the evenings. She is now a freelance writer of self-help articles, cookbook, poems and devotions. Her writing is inspirational for those going through challenging times. Her articles have appeared in other *Moments* books.

Rabbi Frank Stern, PhD, DD, ordained in 1965 at the Hebrew Union College in Cincinnati, Ohio, served for 20 years as Rabbi of Temple Beth Sholom in Santa Ana, California. As Executive Director of the Board of Rabbis of Greater Philadelphia, he headed an agency that provided chaplains to nursing homes, hospitals and prisons in Pennsylvania and New Jersey. Still actively involved in the Central Conference of American Rabbis, Rabbi Stern served as President of the Orange County Board of Rabbis and President of the Pacific Association of Reform Rabbis (seven western states). Until his retirement, Dr.

Stern taught in the Department of Sociology and the Department of Comparative Religion at Cal State University Fullerton. He still teaches at Orange Coast College. Rabbi Stern is the author of the book *A Rabbi Looks at Jesus' Parables*. He lectures extensively throughout California. Rabbi Stern is President of the Orange County Interfaith Network (OCIN), Founder of the Council of Religious Leaders of Orange County and Founding President of the Orange County Jewish Genealogical Society.

Nate Stevens is a "missionary kid" who grew up in a Christian home and church. He has enjoyed a 36-year banking career in a variety of leadership roles. He writes online devotions for Christian Devotions Ministries, devotions for www.SingleMatters.com, and articles for several publications. His book, *Matched 4 Life*, is available at all major book retailers. His next book, *Deck Time with Jesus*, released in January 2018. He has contributed to several *Moments* books (*Divine Moments, Spoken Moments, Christmas Moments, Stupid Moments*, etc.). He is a popular speaker and teacher at conferences, seminars and Bible study groups, speaking on a wide variety of topics. He lives near Charlotte, North Carolina with his beautiful wife, Karen, and is a proud dad of his two awesome kids, Melissa and Mitchell. Contact and book information may be found at: www.natestevens.net.

Annmarie B. Tait resides in Conshohocken, Pennsylvania with her husband, Joe Beck. In addition to writing stories about her large Irish Catholic family and the memories they made, she enjoys singing and recording Irish and American folk songs with her husband. Among her other passions are cooking, sewing and crocheting. Annmarie has over 50 stories published in various anthologies including *Chicken Soup for the Soul* and the *Patchwork Path* series. You may contact her at irishbloom@aol.com.

Myrtle V. Thompson (aka Jenny) is a retired missionary. She and her husband served in Pakistan, Iran, and the UAE. She has also been an educator, a Bible teacher, a writers and women's conference speaker. Now at age 89, she loves gardening in her tiny backyard, has a small ministry visiting the elderly in retirement and rehab facilities, and teaches a Sunday school class of "older folks" (doesn't seem to realize she is in that class, too!). She and her husband, who passed away in 2013, are proud parents of 5 children, 17 grandchildren and 6 great grandchildren.

Beverly Varnado's work has been a finalist for the prestigious Kairos Prize in Screenwriting, a Gideon screenplay finalist, and a semifinalist in Christian Writer's Guild Operation First Novel. She has a screenplay under option as well as two novels in print, *Give My Love to the Chestnut Trees* and *Home to Currahee*. She writes regularly for the *Upper Room Magazine* and her work has been featured on World Radio. She has over 700 posts on her blog, *One Ringing Bell: Peals of words on faith, living, writing and art*. Other anthologies including her work are *Short and Sweet, Short and Sweet Too*, and *Merry Christmas Moments*. To be released in 2018 are a non-fiction book, *Faith in the Fashion District*, the story of how a life on Seventh Avenue launched a lifetime in ministry, and a novel, *The Key to Everything*. Additionally, she works as an artist and recently exhibited at a state university gallery. www. BeverlyVarnado.com, OneRingingBell.blogspot.com.

Mary Ellen Weber enjoys many hobbies including reading, writing, knitting and traveling. She has been writing personal memories that she calls *Mary's Musings* since 2008. She is a member of the Write Group at Wesley Village in Wilmore, Kentucky.

Kathy Whirity is a syndicated newspaper columnist who shares her musings on family life. Kathy is the author of the book, *Life Is a Kaleidoscope*, a compilation of some of her readers' favorite columns. You may reach Kathy by e-mail: kathywhirity@yahoo.com. Her website is www.kathywhirity.com.

Ann Brubaker Greenleaf Wirtz is the author of both *Hand of Mercy* and the Bible study that accompanies her new release. She is a public speaker and group study leader. Ann won the Willie Parker Peace History Book Award from the North Carolina Society of Historians for her book *The Henderson County Curb Market*. Her first book, *Sorrow Answered*, was published in 2006. She was published in *More Christmas Moments, Chicken Soup for the Soul Christmas*, and locally in the *Times-News*, where she has written over 100 articles. She writes a nostalgic remembrance for *The Pulse* each December, featuring her childhood in Webster Groves, Missouri. Ann is the mother of one very dear son and daughter-in-law, and the grandmother of two delightful grandchildren, a girl and a boy. She is married to her beloved Patrick, and they reside in Hendersonville, North Carolina.

Juanita Giberson Woodward is a native of New Jersey, but is currently a resident of Wesley Village Retirement Center in Wilmore, Kentucky. She is a participant in the Village writing group called The Write People. The group leader, Carolyn Roth Barnum, encourages members to be active writers in their areas of interest. Juanita's writing reflects her continued interest in her profession focused on Early Childhood and Special Education, plus poetic humor.

CPSIA information can be obtained
at www.ICGtesting.com
Printed in the USA
FFOW01n0207080618
47046142-49361FF